7⁵⁰J

Merry Xmas Jim
Chapter 3
Your all time fan
Love
Donna Xmas '9?

CAPTAINS

MICHAEL ULMER

Macmillan Canada
Toronto

Canadian Cataloguing in Publication Data

Ulmer, Michael, 1959–
   Captains

Includes index.
ISBN 0–7715–7366–9

1. Toronto Maple Leafs (Hockey team)—Biography.
2. Hockey players—Ontario—Toronto—Biography.
I. Title.

GV848.5A1U55   1995   796.962'092'2713541   C95–931526–8

Macmillan Canada wishes to thank the Canada Council, the Ontario Ministry of Culture and Communications and the Ontario Arts Council for supporting its publishing program.

Macmillan Canada
A Division of Canada Publishing Corporation
Toronto

1 2 3 4 5   99 98 97 96 95

Printed in Canada

CONTENTS

ACKNOWLEDGEMENTS

This book is the product of editor Kirsten Hanson, who conceived and nurtured the idea of a book about the captains of the Toronto Maple Leafs. It survived thanks to Karen O'Reilly's hard work, and because Dan O'Shea and Kevin Von Appin know their way around a computer. It thrived on the generosity of Ted Kennedy, Scott Young, Jim Keon and the staff at the Hockey Hall of Fame.

Like any book, it is also the result of works that came before, specifically books written by Jack Batten, Bill Houston and Scott Young. To all the above and so many more, my thanks.

The author survived due to the abundant patience, love and goodwill of Agnes Bongers with whom I share Sadie and Hannah, the greatest works either of us will ever produce.

To Suzanne LeMoullec,
Taras Dusanowsky and all the people
who love them still.

PROLOGUE

DOUG GILMOUR

CAPTAIN, 1994–Present

August 18, 1994

Doug Gilmour drifts backwards, deflects a puck into the net and raises his arms.

Snow covers his jet black hair as his teammates dart in and out of camera range. His teeth are in place and the smile is genuine, as it always is when Gilmour is spending time with children.

Images from the highlight tape scatter across the screen at the Hockey Hall of Fame: Gilmour playing hockey with neighborhood kids at the local rink, Gilmour in blue and in the NHL, Gilmour fighting, Gilmour hitting, Gilmour scoring.

The Leafs' most visible player since his acquisition from Calgary in January, 1992, Gilmour has scored 351 goals during the regular season, 48 in playoffs goals and by force of will has fashioned himself into one of the National Hockey League's most riveting performers. A Stanley Cup in Calgary and a $15 million contract have cemented his status as a playoff hero and drawing card. Now, with the captaincy of the Toronto Maple Leafs, his ability as leader has been certified.

When Wendel Clark was traded to Quebec in June 1994, Gilmour became the obvious—the only—choice to wear a letter that has graced the left shoulder of 14 players since Conn Smythe hustled enough money to buy the team in 1927 and immediately appointed Hap Day his first captain.

The C has been worn by off-ice jesters and single-minded zealots, by hard drinkers and lifelong abstainers, by womanizers and a Father of the Year.

Smythe is remembered as a dictatorial, union-busting sporting baron, but the line of captains he began has represented the best of what he wanted the Maple Leafs to be.

Smythe built Maple Leaf Gardens in under six months in 1931 and the mix of tenacity, recklessness and courage that went into hockey's finest stage seems to have seeped into the leaders who stride its frozen footboards.

Clearly the C in Toronto stands for character, a single-minded devotion to winning and craft, as much as it stands for captain. Gilmour would be captain even if he weren't the Leafs' best player. George Armstrong, the longest-serving captain in NHL history, didn't spend a day of his term as his team's best player.

Character is the thread that weaves together the stories of 15 very different men. Character has turned a cotton letter sewn onto a jersey into the symbol of heroes.

But the character that defines the captains of the Maple Leafs isn't born in Maple Leaf Gardens. It was forged in a Kingston, Ontario, home and on a Kelvington, Saskatchewan farm, in the gunshot that killed Ted Kennedy's father and even in the smell of horse manure shoveled on wintry mornings by a St. Jacobs' boy named Darryl Sittler.

The C presented to Gilmour by Red Horner at the Hockey Hall of Fame doesn't define Doug Gilmour, just as it didn't define his 14 predecessors.

It is they who have defined the C.

Saturday, February 18, 199
Toronto
Leafs 3–Blues 1

As he's been doing all season, Doug Gilmour arrives at the crease a moment too late. St. Louis Blues' goalie Curtis Joseph is already holding the puck but, looking on from her seat in the reds, Maddison Gilmour is unfazed.

She may be the only person in Maple Leaf Gardens not mesmerized by the sight of Gilmour, but she pays homage in her own way. The Leafs' glossy program sits on her lap and, while her dad toils against the Blues, Maddison borrows a pen from her grandmother, opens the book to a color photo of her father and begins blackening in his front teeth.

Maddison Gilmour is ten years old and the resemblance to her father is most noticeable in her eyes. They too are strikingly brown.

Doug Gilmour loves Maddison with an intensity that dwarfs even the fire he shows on the ice. His devotion to her is reflected in his charitable works which always center on children. His visits to children's hospitals and cancer wards sometimes hit home, and he finds himself touching the temple of his beautiful daughter, willing her to live forever.

To children, Gilmour, elf-like among the giants on the ice, is Peter Pan, and to watch Doug Gilmour at his best, inexhaustible, powered by imagination and unencumbered by size, is to watch a child in joyful play.

But even Peter Pan must grow up. Cancer claimed the lives of two children Gilmour had been visiting over the summer and that experience, along with the labor strife that postponed the season, left Gilmour on edge and cast a cloud over the season.

Maddison's mother, Robyne, and Doug are divorced. Maddison lives with him on weekends but, with the Leafs playing almost every weekend, Maddison spends as much time with Amy Cable, Gilmour's girlfriend, as with her father.

Gilmour and Cable met at the Gardens. Cable was an usher there when Gilmour slipped out of an off-season workout in the Leafs' weight room and asked her out while Cable was working a rock concert. She is 20, 11 years his junior, and her incandescent beauty has landed her many modeling jobs.

The difference in their ages has spawned a stream of rumors of a breakup which peaked during the 103-day lockout. Gilmour recently sold his house in Toronto's Little Portugal and is moving into a condominium with Cable, effectively silencing the gossips for now. Amy, as close in age to Maddison as she is to Doug, fills the child's weekends with crafts, shopping and videos.

Dolly Gilmour sits beside Maddison. In her mid-sixties with a full mane of silver hair, she remains a striking woman. But Doug inherited more than physical beauty from his mother. She is funny, strong-willed and intensely loyal. When asked how Doug lost his four front teeth she answers instantly. April, 1993. Doug was high-sticked by the Chicago Blackhawks' Jeremy Roenick. "And no penalty," she says, the indignation clear two years later.

The Maple Leafs have their latest captain because 50 years earlier, Dolly was a member of the organizing committee for a Sadie Hawkins dance at the Kingston YMCA. True to the conventions of the dance, the boys assembled in the gym before dispersing into nearby streets. The girls gave the boys several minutes head start before rounding them up. Dolly was with three friends when she spied Don Gilmour, also with a group of three, in front of the Y. Three years later, both 18, they were married.

Don teases his wife, saying he could have avoided his fate with a little more speed, but he is a man who knows he did well to be caught. When they watch their son on television, Don shouts for Doug to do more while Dolly shouts at the players bullying her son. They are a formidable pair, two sides of the same coin. Tough-mindedness is a family trait.

The Gilmours are from Kingston and have worked in the prison system that still employs more than 2,000 people in the region. Had he not panned out as a hockey player, Doug Gilmour would probably still be in Kingston, working in the penal industry. Don Gilmour was a storage keeper for 32 years at Kingston Penitentiary. Dolly worked at the staff college and at Joyceville Penitentiary. Both are now retired. Dave, the eldest child, was a recreational worker at Millhaven for ten years but now tends bar at Gilmour's, the family's restaurant. Doug's sister Donna works in security and investigations in the penitentiary service's regional headquarters.

With a stout frame and fleshy features, Don looks comfortable in a hockey jacket. He is, in fact, every inch the hockey parent. Don coached Doug for years and kept him on defense to sharpen the physical aspect of his game, unconcerned that Doug was far too small to play the position. Don never insisted that Dave assert himself physically, and the eldest Gilmour child saw his career stall and die in the World Hockey Association (WHA). Don decided to take more of a role with Doug. He enrolled him in judo to sharpen his reflexes and pulled him out of Junior B when he wasn't getting enough ice time.

This game against the Blues is undistinguished for Gilmour, one of a handful already this season. The acceleration and anticipation of the play that marked his first two seasons in Toronto are nowhere in evidence, but the captain's lack of production is ignored in the ease with which the Leafs dispatch the talented if road-weary Blues. Although Gilmour earns an assist, only his second point in five games, he is not a factor in the contest.

After the game, the Gilmours chat with some of Doug's Kingston cousins. Don and Dolly will stay with Doug until after Monday's game against Detroit. Maddison is having the most fun she's had all night, skipping with Mike Gartner's daughter, Natalie, in the catacombs of the Gardens.

Monday, February 20, 1995
Toronto
Detroit 4–Toronto 2

Dave Andreychuk, a slow skater with a safecracker's nimble hands, has been Gilmour's principal on-ice foil since being traded from Buffalo for Grant Fuhr in February, 1993. When Gilmour would take a defenseman wide, Andreychuk would lumber for the net. When Gilmour would attack a scrum, Andreychuk would reach into the scrum, corral the loose puck and flip it home.

But if the lockout was damaging to Gilmour, it was crippling to Andreychuk who is rumored to have showed up for the one-week training camp 15 pounds over his ideal playing weight. Suddenly Andreychuk's skating has dropped from poor to plodding. The other member of Gilmour's line, right-winger Nikolai Borschevsky, is a willing but undersized forward who has been manhandled through the early going.

Gilmour is first and foremost a playmaker. He isn't big enough to overpower a goalie or defenseman in close, or strong enough to blast a shot from the perimeter. At about 5'10" and 165 pounds, he is slight, almost chicken-chested, but strong in the neck and shoulders. After years of masking his build, he remains modest, invariably layered in at least two towels in the dressing room. But no amount of subterfuge could convince onlookers Gilmour's physique is even remotely similar to Vancouver's well-muscled Pavel Bure or Detroit's Steve Yzerman.

Like Wayne Gretzky, Gilmour plays a game built on thoughtfulness and intelligence, and when he plays it well his lack of physical strength is irrelevant. Former captain Wendel Clark can turn a game around with a bodycheck. He can punch a player into submission or rip a 40-foot shot past a goalie. While Doug Gilmour is courageous and chippy on ice, he can do none of those things. He is particularly dependent on the play of his linemates, and with a too-slow Andreychuk and too-small Borschevsky, Gilmour's contribution is limited.

To inject some offense into the line, coach Pat Burns has occasionally dropped Andreychuk in favor of Mats Sundin (although the move chokes off whatever chances Andreychuk is enjoying). Gilmour's game has thrived when he has been teamed with Sundin, but the idea behind acquiring the big Swede was to supplement Gilmour at center, not pile the team's most talented offensive players onto one line.

Hamstrung, Burns has reunited the Andreychuk-Gilmour-Borschevsky line for this game but, when a bouncing puck finds a Detroit player and the trio lags a zone behind for the game's opening goal, Burns has had enough. Ray Sheppard's goal triggers a ten-minute benching of the Gilmour line, a fact not lost on the Maple Leafs' fans.

In the reds, Don Gilmour is livid. "Maybe he's not scoring, but benching Doug isn't the way to get him going," he says. "He still does all the other things no other player does, all over the ice."

Gilmour's all-around game is the foundation of his leadership. While his offense has made him a fan favorite, it's his defense, or more specifically the caliber of his defense considering his offensive numbers, that has made him one of the

league's best players. Gilmour is always in motion. His quickness and desire help him move back into action just moments
after he seems trapped deep in the offensive zone. His defensive prowess is especially eye-catching considering he often
sets up shop behind the opposition's goal rather than high in
the slot.

Gilmour won the Frank Selke Trophy for defensive excellence in 1993 and last season finished as the runner-up for the
same award. He goes into the corners fearlessly and, when he
applies himself, is excellent on face-offs. Like Detroit's Sergei
Fedorov, Gilmour is a dual threat. He shadows the opposition's
most gifted offensive player while exploiting the gaps in
defense offensive players invariably allow.

But even Gilmour's defensive game has been unexceptional
this season. His ability to anticipate plays and create turnovers
and neutral zone interceptions has been missing. The fans
cheer when Gilmour returns ten minutes later but his presence
has little impact on the game. Pucks that used to find his stick
click off his heel. His passes hit teammates slightly off-stride,
and the player he is checking always seems to have gotten rid
of the puck before Gilmour can create a turnover.

That he misses an empty net is of little concern. While
Gilmour is accurate with his shot, he has been bad at putting
the puck into empty nets throughout his career. But it is of
great concern that the Leafs, revamped in the off-season, seem
light years away from the cohesive unit of past years. The
team, so clearly Gilmour's over the last two years, looks rud-
derless. Sundin, not Gilmour, is now the club's most dynamic
player.

With about three minutes left and the Leafs down by one,
Gilmour hits Paul Coffey during a delayed offside. It's a tough
play but not a dirty one, merely a breach of etiquette between
two of the game's premier talents, but what follows is an

atypical display of thoughtless hockey. Coffey punches
Gilmour in the head and Gilmour looks to get a call from referee Kerry Fraser. When there is no whistle, Gilmour drops
his gloves and attacks Coffey. He spends the rest of the game
in the locker room, and the Leafs surrender an empty net goal
and lose 4–2.

Doug Gilmour will fight when angry. In his third year of
Junior A hockey in Cornwall, he was determined to prove he
deserved better than the seventh-round spot by which the St.
Louis Blues acquired him. Early in that season, he dropped his
gloves against Kitchener Rangers tough guy Mike Eagles, one
of the league's best fighters and a player more surprised than
anyone that Gilmour wanted to fight. A left hand from Eagles
broke Gilmour's nose and quickly ended the bout.

Instead of his fists, Gilmour does most of his damage with
his stick. "If fighting was illegal," he once quipped to a friend,
"I'd be the toughest guy in the league." In 1992, he slashed Los
Angeles forward Tomas Sandstrom and broke his arm. Suspen-
sion for eight non-game days cost him $30,000 in lost salary
but solidified his reputation as the nastiest high-scoring player
in the game.

Burns' post-game media scrum lasts only a few moments. He
states the obvious—the Gilmour line was benched for the
defensive transgression—but offers no further explanation. Nor
does Gilmour. It's Amy's birthday and before the media can
find him, the captain is on his way to a cross-town nightclub.

Tuesday, February 21, 1995
Toronto

The Leafs are scheduled to practice at noon and fly to
Detroit at 4 p.m. After a 75-minute workout that focuses
mainly on finding the centre or the supporting defenseman on

the breakout, Gilmour appears for the media, delaying his shower so that he can explain to groups of reporters that, no, he isn't doubting his abilities, and, no, he isn't going to quit trying.

"It's not frustrating. I've been coping with slumps like this for 12 years," Gilmour tells a television reporter. "It will come."

Despite the previous night's loss, which drops the Leafs to .500, the dressing room mood is light. Burns will use Gartner instead of Borschevsky on Gilmour's right in Detroit. Asked what the 35-year-old Gartner brings to the line, Gilmour answers, "Age."

He sidesteps questions about last night's benching. "My job is just to go out and play. Burnsie is the guy who dictates what happens."

But no amount of next-day diplomacy can disguise the fact that, after a week of unflagging praise and public patience, Burns benched his captain's line. It was the first time in nearly three seasons Gilmour had been held out and, while Burns told reporters before the practice that the benching had been a message to the line and not to one player, the implications of the move were clear. With more than a third of the 48-game season gone, the coach is tired of waiting for results. Already Burns had begun to take some of the premier ice time away from Gilmour's line. Gilmour has spent much less time on killing penalties this year, and Mike Eastwood has replaced Gilmour as the number one choice to take a key face-off.

If this pains Gilmour, he will not say so. Gilmour banters with the media far more easily than Clark did, but his comments aren't much more revealing. If Clark was a closed man, then Gilmour is an *open* closed man. He is personable and forthcoming but not insightful.

Amy Cable mentions that reserve first when describing Gilmour. "I don't know half the time what his inner feelings really are. He will say to the press, everybody, his parents, me, 'No, no, this doesn't bother me.' But you can tell that it does. He's just not the type of person who would ever say anything."

The truth is, Doug Gilmour has endured a lousy eight months.

The two principal passions of Gilmour's life are children and hockey and over the last few months he has lost both.

He was powerless to stop Vancouver's five-game victory over Toronto in last year's semi-final. Then, the lockout took the joy from an off-season that included his coronation as captain at the Hockey Hall of Fame.

Tired of the stalled negotiations between the National Hockey League Players' Association (NHLPA) and the NHL owners, Gilmour bolted for Switzerland in November. In nine games with Rapperswill of the Swiss League, he scored twice and added 15 assists but was frustrated by the officiating that robbed him of his natural inclination to instigate. He did not return after Christmas.

Even more disturbing was the death over the summer of Janel Selby, a child Gilmour had met five years before while visiting a children's hospital in Calgary. Gilmour attended the funeral and stayed at the Selby house the night before the little girl was buried.

Janel's death, along with the death of another young child he had befriended only a couple of weeks earlier, hit Gilmour hard. He could comfort the children and the family, and his celebrity and his willingness to help allowed him inside tightly knit families. But once there, he felt the same helplessness as everyone else does when confronted by a fatal disease.

Gilmour grieved for Janel Selby and lashed out when criticized by the organizer of a charity golf tournament he missed while attending the funeral. "I couldn't believe it," Gilmour said, his voice dropping to a low murmur. "Here this person was worried about a golf tournament when a little girl was dying."

Death has shaped Doug Gilmour. The illusion of immortality, so common to young people, was lost forever when he was 17 and his cousin, Mike Anson, also 17, died from a rare form of cancer. The sight of his cousin, emaciated and carried by his parents, was an image that Doug Gilmour could not comprehend and cannot forget.

"It's kind of amazing. You're young, you take things for granted. You never think that tomorrow you might die. Here's my cousin, we saw each other at least once a week, a great kid, always healthy. Within a year, he weighs 60 pounds and his parents are carrying him around, bathing him. I kept on asking my dad why. I could never figure it out."

A few weeks after Anson's death, Mike Callaghan, the young brother of a close friend, lost his life in a snowmobile accident.

"When Mike passed away, that was a little wake-up call that life was something that was important. Those things change you," Gilmour said. "If I died tomorrow, I'd just say thank you because I had a great life. What I can't believe is when you go into kids' hospitals and see kids fighting for their lives who haven't had a chance to live."

Professional sports is dominated by an accelerated life cycle. NHL careers are usually born when a player is in his early twenties and dead within a decade. Every additional year in the league is a struggle to keep alive a fairy-tale life of wealth, fame and privilege. Because of his size, Gilmour has always had to fight for that life and he is acutely conscious of how much time he has left. His age pops into conversation and he often jokes about his seniority.

Doug Gilmour always wanted to make his mark as a hockey player. He played against kids three and four years older, often giving away a foot and more than 50 pounds. At 16, desperate for more ice time, Gilmour traveled to Belleville to play for the Tier II Bulls. Bulls' coach Larry Mavety knew Gilmour was small but he couldn't believe his eyes when he saw his 129-pound rushing defenseman.

Belleville gave Gilmour more than just a chance to play. The Bulls used an Olympic-sized ice surface and with more room to maneuver Gilmour learned to extend his stride and improve his skating. Late in the season, when injuries had taken their toll on his forwards, Mavety moved Gilmour to forward.

Gilmour was drafted that summer by the Ontario Hockey League's Cornwall Royals as a centre and the career clock began ticking in earnest. He had seen firsthand that life doesn't go on forever but Gilmour decided he would jam whatever he could into whatever time he had. No one would tell him he was too small to go into a corner or a scrum in front of the net.

On or off the ice, he would do anything for an edge. When he played for the Royals, Gilmour taped small weights around his waist during weigh-ins and covered them with shorts to convince scouts he was five pounds heavier. He became an expert at lifting his heel when his height was measured.

With the Royals, Gilmour was walking into a powerhouse. They were the Memorial Cup champions in 1980 and Dale Hawerchuk was ensconced as the team's resident superstar. When the Royals returned to the Memorial Cup that season, it was Gilmour who scored the Cup winner against Kitchener.

Because of his size, his rookie OHL season wasn't enough to get Gilmour drafted into the NHL. His response was a 46-goal, 119-point season the following year. Gilmour was chosen this time by the St. Louis Blues, but only in the seventh round. Gilmour considered this spot another snub and he returned to Cornwall for the 1982–83 season more determined than ever to dominate.

"The second year, I was a little heartbroken as far as being chosen, what, 134th overall, seventh round?" he said. "That was another little wake-up call."

In his third year, Gilmour set Ontario Hockey League records with 107 assists and 177 points, and racked up a league record 55-game point streak. He also met Robyne Dunham. Dunham, a student nurse in Cornwall, was 23, four years older than Doug. The two were married in St. Louis a few years later. Gilmour has said that marrying Robyne helped his career by keeping him at home and off the fast track.

"It was positive for my career that I was married when I was young," he told a *Toronto Life* reporter. "I needed somebody to go home to, somebody to put their foot down and tell me, 'You're not doing that.'" Two years later, when Doug was 22, Maddison was born.

Tuesday, February 22, 1995
Detroit, 9:10 a.m.

Doug Gilmour has a weakness for practical jokes. Once, while playing for the Cornwall Royals, he was hospitalized with a suspected concussion. Trainer Steve Ouderkirk went to the hospital after the game and asked to see Gilmour. Moments later, he was greeted by a somber priest who asked Ouderkirk to follow him. Naturally, Ouderkirk presumed the worst.

"I was going out of my mind by the time we reached the cubicle but, when we got there, there was Doug, sitting up, killing himself laughing," Ouderkirk said. "He had talked the priest into setting the whole thing up."

When tiny puncture holes are found in a glass in the Leafs' dressing room or Vaseline has been pushed into a jelly doughnut, Gilmour is usually the culprit.

Over a breakfast of fresh fruit, orange juice and granola in the hotel, he relates his latest prank. He and Amy started a rumor that she was pregnant. It took an hour to sweep through the Gardens and get back to them.

Because of the difference in their ages, Cable's employment as an usher and her great beauty, interest in the couple around Maple Leaf Gardens is profound. It annoys them both but over breakfast he answers questions about Cable without hesitation.

"Amy and I get along great but we go through lots of stages to make sure the relationship is strong, that's all," Gilmour said. "That's what we're doing now. We love each other. The odds are we'll be together. She's a good girl, she wants everything I want, to start all over, to have more children. She's not one that wants to hang at the bars all night. She wants a family. That means a lot. I can talk to her."

The age gap, he said, doesn't matter. "She's 20. She hasn't had the experience I've had in life, she hasn't seen the things and relationships I've gone through. But she surprises the heck out of me every day."

Cable, for her part, loves Gilmour. "He's taught me a lot," she volunteers, but while she is young, she is also shrewd. She understands what motivates him.

"He wants to leave his mark. From when he was told he was too small, he's gotten this little edge to him. He knows he's going to have to retire sometime, but he wants people to go, 'Yeah, that's the Doug Gilmour card I have. God, he was good.' He wants there to be something about him so he's still there."

Gilmour's chance to begin making that mark did not come easily. In the summer of 1984, he arrived at the NHL draft in Montreal to talk contract with the Blues. The club was about to be sold by the owners, Ralston Purina, and the top bidder was a consortium from Saskatchewan. The NHL, horrified by the prospect of moving the team from an American television market to the Saskatchewan wheat belt, threatened to block the sale until a new owner was found.

Although Harry Ornest arrived to save the Blues, Gilmour, anxious to play while the team reorganized, accepted an offer to play that winter in Dusseldorf, Germany.

Gilmour arrived in time for an intrasquad game for charity and found a world radically different from the one to which he was accustomed.

"It was get-to-know-your-player night," he recalls, laughing. "They gave me a puck and a rose. You go out, you throw the puck in the stands on one side, take the rose to another side, give it to a lady and give her a kiss. Then you sit down on a seat at centre ice. A guy goes up, spray paints your name, holds it up to one side and then holds it up to another side to the crowd."

Within a couple of weeks, the Blues were solvent and Gilmour was ready to come home. "Don't sign anything, even an autograph," advised Don. "There may be a [European] contract underneath it."

Gilmour signed with the Blues for $80,000 per season and began the process of establishing himself as an NHL player.

"He was, at best, a long shot," then Blues coach Jacques Demers has said. The Blues were already solid at centre. The prolific Bernie Federko held down the number-one spot and a truckload of role players—Blake Dunlop, Mike Zuke, Guy Chouinard and Alain Lemieux, Mario's brother—were fighting it out for spot duty. There seemed to be little room for an undersized and inexperienced forward.

Gilmour quickly saw he would have to break into the league as a defensive centre. Demers, a rookie coach, was looking for somebody who made an impression. Gilmour, through unceasing work in training camp, made Demers' choice easy.

"I went in there to make that team, and it didn't matter what it was going to take," Gilmour said. "Jacques Demers wanted something new to come into that team. He was new, the general manager was new, the owner was new and when they saw me, they saw a fresh face. Plus, they didn't have anybody in the minors. They had to try and give me a shot."

Gilmour played all 80 games and learned firsthand the on-ice habits of superstars.

"Overall, Jacques made me a better player by having me learn how to play against a Wayne Gretzky, a Marcel Dionne, a Denis Savard," Gilmour said. "They're all different and unique in their own way and to go out and do this, to me, was just the challenge I needed."

Since the game's greatest offensive talents are often deficient defensively, Gilmour was also able to exploit the ample chances he enjoyed. He finished his rookie season with 25 goals.

Demers did Gilmour another favor. He roomed his rookie centre with captain Brian Sutter, the Blues' inspirational captain and leader. "Brian had a big influence on Doug," Demers said.

"Brian Sutter exemplified a captain," Gilmour said. "He was a guy who, when he was hurt, was going to play. A guy that you'd want on your team and who would go through the boards for you. I said, I'm going to play for this guy. If I don't play for this guy, he's going to kill me."

It was Sutter, struck by the fury in Gilmour's eyes, who nicknamed him Killer and, while Gilmour has enjoyed a career chockful of great playoffs, the 1994 post-season was the one in which he best emulated his mentor. Gilmour played the play-offs with a severely sprained ankle, enduring regular pain killers, but refused to come out of the lineup. "Some guys should be embarrassed to be in the same dressing room," Burns said after the playoffs.

In 1986 Sutter missed half of the regular season and all of the playoffs. Gilmour garnered more ice time and along with Federko led the league in playoff points. He recorded five assists in one game alone, a series-deciding game against

Minnesota in which light-scoring Greg Paslawski scored three times, all on glorious feeds from Gilmour. Federko called it "the best single game performance I've ever seen."

In 1986 Demers bolted for Detroit, and Jacques Martin, a coach with a less restrictive offensive philosophy, was named his successor. All elements were now in place for Gilmour's breakout season. Federko talked to him after his first shift in the first preseason game. "We need you this year. Nobody has seen what you can do before."

They soon would. Gilmour doubled his goal total from 22 to 45 and cracked the hundred-point barrier for the first time. He followed that season up with 86 points in 1987–88, but scandal soon ended Gilmour's tenure with the Blues.

In June, 1988 a St. Louis couple told the Blues that Gilmour had sexually assaulted their daughter, Maddison's babysitter, on several occasions. Gilmour was 24; the girl was 13. The family asked the Blues for $200,000 in damages. When they were rebuffed, they filed a $1 million civil suit against Doug and Robyne, saying she knew about the assault. The couple also sued the Blues, claiming the team had reneged on an offer to pay compensation.

Gilmour denied any wrongdoing and with Robyne filed a $4 million countersuit claiming libel and slander. A grand jury ruled there was insufficient evidence to file any criminal charges against Gilmour and, in the end, both civil suits were dropped.

Soon afterward, the Blues, aware that the negative publicity could undermine one of their top assets, decided to trade Gilmour. Cliff Fletcher, the general manager of the Calgary Flames, stepped up and pulled off the first of his two career thefts of Doug Gilmour. He was dealt, along with Mark Hunter, Steve Bozek and Michael Dark, to Calgary for Mike Bullard, Craig Coxe and Tim Corkery. This trade would rank as perhaps the most one-sided of all time were it not for the Flames repeating the Blues' error three seasons later with an even more lopsided deal.

The Flames won their first and only Cup in 1988–89, Gilmour's first year. As part of his contribution, Gilmour scored two third-period goals in game six, including the Stanley Cup winner against Montreal.

Still, the Flames were not Gilmour's team. Lanny McDonald was the most popular Flame, Joe Nieuwendyk was the club's offensive powerhouse and Joel Otto was invariably coach Terry Crisp's first choice to take a key face-off. Gilmour was still clearly a leader. Following McDonald's retirement, he was part of a rotating captaincy with Otto and Jamie Macoun.

Gilmour was an absurd luxury in Calgary. One of the game's best two-way players, he gave the Flames depth and versatility but, as the 1991 season opened, Gilmour was determined that he would earn what he felt he deserved. The Flames and Gilmour's agent, Larry Kelly, battled over both salary and the length of the contract but, when they couldn't reach an agreement, the dispute moved into arbitration. Gilmour asked for $1.2 million and four years; the Flames countered with $550,000 and three years.

Arbitration is one of the most curious processes in sport. Teams that devote countless hours to building up a player's image savage the same player before an arbitrator who has the authority to side with the player, the team, or, as happened with Gilmour, come down somewhere in the middle.

But this time the process, intended to smooth over acrimony, did the exact opposite. By the time the arbitration was in full swing, Fletcher had left for Toronto and Doug Risebrough had moved from coach to coach/general manager. Risebrough and the Flames based their argument on Gilmour's age. They claimed that at 29, his skills were beginning to fade, and, indeed, his goal total had fallen in each of his three seasons with the Flames from 26 to 24 to 20.

But while Gilmour's point totals were somewhat lower, the players on Gilmour's wings, with few defensive responsibilities thanks to Gilmour's excellent defensive skills, prospered with his arrival. Theoren Fleury and Joe Mullen enjoyed excellent seasons playing with Gilmour.

Gilmour was awarded $750,000 but whatever future he had in Calgary was destroyed.

"In retrospect, I don't know that the solution couldn't have been found earlier," Risebrough said. "I never considered it a personal thing. The player was looking for more recognition and we weren't in a position to do it. The arbitration process can work, the whole purpose of it is to reconcile the two parties, but in this case, it didn't happen."

Gilmour concedes that the salary standoff was a war between two unbending men.

"I think the biggest thing is, Doug Risebrough is a good man. We didn't see eye to eye. We're very similar in the way we play the game. We were both maybe hotheaded at times, we both wanted to compete. Maybe that took our negotiations and got them out of hand."

Doug Gilmour decided to hasten a trade and, after a win on New Year's Eve against Montreal, he quit the Calgary Flames. Although in typical fashion he played one of his best games of the season, scoring a goal and an assist in the 3–2 victory, he was eviscerated in the media.

Fletcher, sensitive to the goings-on in his old territory, squared off with Risebrough. The Flames were on the edge; despite a talented core of players, they had been unable to repeat their Stanley Cup success of 1989. In his first seven months on the job, Risebrough had fallen short in his attempts to bring Pat LaFontaine or Brent Sutter to Calgary, and Edmonton had moved first and landed Dave Manson, another player the Flames coveted.

The Flames' primary concern was to land a right-winger so they could move Theoren Fleury back to centre. The Leafs had an extra right-winger in Gary Leeman, a player only two seasons removed from a 50-goal year. Risebrough and Fletcher bartered quickly; within hours of Gilmour's walkout, they had negotiated a ten-player deal: Gilmour, Jamie Macoun, Ric Nattress, Rick Wamsley and Kent Manderville from Calgary for Gary Leeman, Craig Berube, Alexander Godynyuk, Michel Petit and Jeff Reese from Toronto.

The Maple Leafs' fans were ecstatic but it would soon prove a staggeringly poor trade for the Flames. "Obviously," Risebrough concedes, "it did not work out."

Leeman continued his freefall and, after only 59 games and 11 goals with Calgary, was peddled for Brian Skrudland to Montreal. A couple of seasons later, Berube was traded to Washington for a fifth-round draft choice. Godynyuk was a washout with the Flames and was claimed by Florida in the expansion draft. Petit was a middle of the pack defenseman who is now playing in Los Angeles and Reese appeared in only 39 regular season games with the Flames before being dispatched to Hartford.

On the other side of the ledger, Macoun has extended a good career in Toronto, Manderville is a role player and Wamsley spent two years as a backup and mentor to Felix Potvin before retiring to become a Leafs coach. Nattress signed as a free agent with Philadelphia after a partial season in Toronto but injuries forced him to retire.

In Calgary, Doug Gilmour jumped around his house when

he learned of the deal. He scored his first goal with the Leafs just a few minutes into his first game, beating Detroit's Greg Millen on January 3, 1992, at the Joe Louis Arena.

Now, three years later, he was back in Detroit and everything Gilmour could have dreamed of when he demanded the trade has come to pass.

Tuesday, February 2, 1995
Detroit
Detroit 4–Leafs 1

Another Motown hit plays from the speakers above the scoreboard and Gilmour uses the commercial break to adjust his skates.

During the off-season surgeons shaved protruding bones in Gilmour's feet and the surgery has changed their landscape, leaving nerves vulnerable to the pressure of tight skates. Occasionally, his feet become numb and the loosening and retying of his skates isn't so much a nervous habit as a chance to relieve the pressure.

Gilmour's constant fiddling and tightening created the problem in the first place, and irritated bone responded by manufacturing more calcium, making the problem worse.

Gilmour is a particular man. He cuts down shin pads with surgical scissors to lighten them and uses the thinnest shoulder pads available. For better passing, he uses a stick that is virtually straight. He tucks in his jersey on the left side, in homage to Wayne Gretzky, but, if he wants to change his luck, changes sides or slides the entire jersey in his pants. But on this night, no altered ritual will end his slump.

Andreychuk gets a gift goal when a Todd Gill shot hits a Detroit player and the puck lands on his stick in the slot but a giveaway by Macoun leads to Shawn Burr's winner early in the second period. The Red Wings check conscientiously and cruise to a 4–1 win.

Gilmour has only one point in his last five games and has not scored in seven. He takes solace in the fact that his skating is still strong. "I'd be worried if I wasn't skating but the puck just isn't coming to me."

Fans, and sometimes writers, think that a player who isn't successful isn't trying. Players and coaches know better. Most players give their maximum or near it on most nights—it's what they have to give that varies.

Professional athletes see their game as almost a life form unto itself. When a player says he'll work hard and continue to press, he is applying the only known remedy to a slump. He is also recognizing that for whatever reason, the game has turned away from him and he can only wait for it to come back.

Because of the difficulties with his linemates, because of the changes to his body over the last eight months, because of the surgery on his feet, because of the lockout, because of a dozen potential reasons, the game that Doug Gilmour has played brilliantly eludes him now the way a leaf, blown from its branch, eludes a child who tries to catch it. The harder Gilmour tries, the less chance he seems to have of being in the right place.

"The best way to describe what's happening to a lot of us, not just Doug, is if you think about a batter in baseball," offers Mike Ridley, a thoughtful veteran. "It just seems like the ball is coming a little bit faster, and, when you swing, you do a little something wrong. But the only thing you can do is keep on swinging. It's something that's unexplained in sport and it's tough to take."

When he was younger, slumps consumed Doug Gilmour. He would curse and kick the boards, convinced that if only he tried harder he could change his fate. The years have taught him differently. Hockey, for those who know it, is fickle above all.

"It seems like such a simple game but it's not," Gilmour said over breakfast. "You make it harder than it is. You have to try and have the confidence to play hard every night even though you can't be successful every night. When I was younger, I didn't get that. I couldn't understand how I would do the same thing and be successful one night and not the other night."

This is Gilmour's first real slump in Toronto since he arrived from Calgary with both skates churning. Gilmour scored 15 goals and recorded 49 points in 40 games after the trade. The following season under new coach Pat Burns, the Leafs upped their points total by 32.

Gilmour, now 30, was in top form. He signed a five-year, $15 million contract with the Leafs. His 127-point regular season was only his second 100-point campaign and it bettered by 22 points his previous career best. In his first full year in Toronto, he set new team records for points and assists. Gilmour's quarter-final overtime goal against the Blues' Curtis Joseph, a behind-the-net classic in which he juked to his left, crossed over and stuffed the puck past the highly regarded goalie, was the high-water mark of a 21-game playoff run. Gilmour's 25 assists were the best of the playoffs and his 35 post-season points were bettered only by Wayne Gretzky. At plus 16, Gilmour was the best plus-minus player in the post-season.

Gilmour lost weight steadily throughout the playoffs and his blackened eyes made him look even more emaciated. When he gave Gilmour a day off, an admiring Burns said, "Dougie has gone back to his home planet to rest."

The 1993–94 season was more of the same: a 111-point regular season followed by a 28-point playoff splurge over 18 games. The high point was Gilmour's four-assist performance that tied the second-round series against San Jose. Wendel Clark and Gilmour, playing with a severely sprained ankle, were the Leafs' two best players but the team's lack of depth proved fatal in the five-game series loss to Vancouver in the quarter-finals.

That same lack of depth led to Clark's trade to the Quebec Nordiques. The deal, unveiled at the 1994 entry draft, saw Clark, Sylvain Lefebvre and highly touted prospect Landon Wilson go to the Nordiques for Mats Sundin, Garth Butcher and prospect Todd Warriner.

Written off countless times as too small and twice traded, Doug Gilmour was now the premier player in one of the league's showcase markets and the captain of a proud, reinvigorated team. He had proven wrong scouts and armchair observers who said he couldn't survive in the NHL because of his size.

"That's always something that's driven me more, when people say you can't do it," Gilmour said. "It makes me want to do it more. I think I've been fortunate the way my career has gone, that people have said I was too small."

Gilmour, like Sutter before him, is an inspiring example in the dressing room.

"Brian was perfect for the job because he gave such a big effort," Gilmour noted. "The players had such respect for him that they felt they were cheating him if they didn't give their best all the time."

It is a description similar to those accorded Gilmour.

"The captains I've had on my teams, Bob Gainey and Guy Carbonneau in Montreal, Wendel Clark here, were quiet guys who led by example and made speeches only at the right time," Burns told the press on the day Gilmour was made captain. "Gilmour is there every game, every practice, with a top effort. His leadership will be by example."

"Quite frankly, Doug is the type of person, I think, who can handle it [the job] with ease," said Fletcher. "It sounds corny, but it's almost as if he's been training for a role like this his entire career."

Thursday, February 23, 1995
Toronto
Leafs 3–Mighty Ducks 1

For tonight's game against the Mighty Ducks, Doug Gilmour needs some time for contemplation. He does not attend the game day skate. Instead he stays at home and watches himself on video. The team has prepared a highlight package and Gilmour studies his movements, determined to replicate them tonight.

In the first period, Gilmour serves notice that he is piecing his game back together. He calls a play in the face-off circle, positions Terry Yake and wins the draw cleanly. Yake rattles a shot past Guy Hebert and the Leafs lead 1–0.

With two minutes to play in the period and the Leafs enjoying a power play, Gilmour wriggles away from his check for a split second and veers toward the Ducks' net. Sundin finds him from the corner and Gilmour redirects the puck under the crossbar before Hebert can move. The drought is over.

Gilmour's passes hit the tape; his skating seems imperceptibly better. He finishes with a goal and an assist, wins 17 of 25 face-offs and the Leafs coast to a 3–1 win.

Saturday, February 25, 1995
Toronto
Leafs 5–Jets 2

Doug Gilmour is deep in the Winnipeg end. His stick cradles the puck. The Leafs are clinging to a 3–2 lead and, in the eye of the storm, Gilmour waits.

He drifts toward Winnipeg goaltender Tim Cheveldae who, anticipating the shot, glides out to within a few feet of Gilmour. Even without benefit of the replay, the play seems to take forever. Milliseconds pass while the defenders close in. Gilmour slides the puck into the slot for a streaking Sundin. The pass is perfect; Sundin rifles the puck into the unoccupied cage.

For the Jets, it's a backbreaking goal. For the Leafs, a game clincher orchestrated by their on-ice leader, a signal that after a slow start perhaps that magic sense of the game has returned to Doug Gilmour.

"You can see him coming along," says Burns, visibly relieved.

Gilmour slips out of the trainer's room after the game and, half dressed, begins autographing a stick, a cap, a jersey and a picture for a little boy. Only when the boy takes his cap off is it clear that he has lost his hair to chemotherapy.

The media are coming now, having left Dave Ellett for fresh quotes from Gilmour. This time, there will be relief when he speaks, but before they arrive, he turns to the child and puts his hand on his shoulder. "I'll see you again, OK, buddy?" says the captain of the Toronto Maple Leafs.

CHAPTER 1

HAP DAY

CAPTAIN 1927–1937

C larence "Hap" Day was the first and most influential captain of the Toronto Maple Leafs, the model which 14 future leaders would follow, the most valuable employee Conn Smythe ever hired.

Day, who died in 1990 at the age of 88, was an employee of the Maple Leafs for 29 years, the only person to captain, coach and manage the team. Smythe and Day were equally responsible for building the Leafs; to discuss one alone is to do a disservice to the other.

Day reigned as the team's on-ice leader from its first Bull season as the Maple Leafs in 1927–28, until 1936–37. During this period, they finished first three times and made four trips to the Stanley Cup finals. In 1932, Day scored three playoff goals as the Leafs took home the Stanley Cup.

A superb captain made an even better coach. He handled the Leafs from 1940 to 1950, a decade in which they won five Stanley Cups. Hap Day was the first NHL coach to win three cups in a row. And, while he is listed as the club's general manager only for the 1957–58 season, Day, the assistant GM to Smythe for nearly a decade, helped manage the team from

1950–58. In all, Hap Day captained, coached or managed in seven of the Leafs' 11 Stanley Cup-winning seasons.

Clarence Day had long since become "Hap" by the time he reached Maple Leaf Gardens. A custodian in his public school, one of many charmed by the boy's cheerfulness and industry, gave Clarence Day the nickname he would carry his whole life. The name would later seem ironic. As a coach, Day was frequently pensive during good times and sullen and withdrawn after a loss.

In many ways, he was Smythe's opposite. As a player, Day was carefree and a rabid practical joker while the hard-minded Smythe had no time or interest in jokes.

Smythe was a small man. As an amateur hockey player he was a pesky and intense competitor who compensated for his size with desire. Day's athleticism seemed effortless by comparison. He was a scratch golfer and an excellent ballplayer. At 5'11" and 175 pounds, he was half a foot taller and 40 pounds heavier than Smythe.

Smythe was a dapper dresser who favored spats and who liked to make an impression. Day dressed conservatively and to the end of his life lived frugally. Although he retired from business a wealthy man, Day insisted on driving the same car, a 1976 Lincoln Continental, for the final 14 years of his life. "Why should I buy a new car," he liked to tell his son Kerry, "when I'm not going to be around long enough to use it."

Smythe was open, bombastic and generous. Day was often taciturn.

"Smythe was a very personable person, far more so than Hap Day," said Red Horner, one of Day's teammates. "Hap Day was much more cool. He didn't have the personality Smythe did."

Smythe loved to needle Day about his habit of using words he didn't understand. The habit was most conspicuous at Day's wedding when he began his speech, "Now that we have consummated the marriage."

Day's attitude toward Smythe was respectful but not reverential. Day often referred to Smythe as "Mussy," a variation of Mussolini.

"I don't think Day ever had any real affection for Smythe," said the *Toronto Star*'s Milt Dunnell, who knew both men well, "but he had admiration for him."

The two were similar in all the ways that mattered. Like Smythe, Day eschewed alcohol and tobacco. The Maple Leafs forbade alcohol on the train, a rule that ran against the league norm. Day had a policy of sticking his finger into the champagne-filled Stanley Cup and tasting it, but that dip marked the beginning and the end of his drinking.

Both men were intense, prodigious workers with a common intuition. From his regular seat in the greens, Smythe would summon a runner, often an injured player, to give Day instructions such as whom to bench. Invariably, by the time the messenger reached the bench, the offending player would already be sitting on it.

"I don't know if Day studied Smythe and set a pattern for himself or if it was the other way around," *Toronto Star* sports editor Andy Lytle wrote in 1947. "The point to remember, if you are interested that is, could be that nature cast both in a mould which might have been fashioned by a high priest of the ancient Spartans."

Clarence Day was born in Owen Sound, Ontario, in 1901 but grew up in Midland, Ontario, with his brother and twin sisters.

The children thrived under the care of their mother, Elizabeth. Day's father, Sid, ran a hotel and later worked for Canadian Pacific Railroad, but he was often absent. When he was home, he was often drunk. Sid Day's alcoholism was the reason his son never imbibed.

"My father had seen enough damage done," said Hap's son, Kerry. "My grandfather wasn't drinking all his life but there was a period of time, in a crucial growing-up period of my dad's life, that he was. I think that had to be the influence on his life that convinced my dad not to drink."

Initially, Day refused when the coach of the Midland high school team asked him to play. A spot on the team meant scratching together $2.75 for a team sweater and Day didn't have the money. A family friend stepped in and bought the sweater, and Day's hockey career was off the ground.

Still, Day never considered a professional career. He played amateur hockey with the Midland Juniors and senior hockey with the Hamilton Tigers. Hockey gave him enough money to attend the University of Toronto where he spent three years gaining a degree in pharmacy.

Day was approached about signing with the local professional team, the Toronto St. Pats, by one of the club's owners, a man named Charlie Querrie. But Day was a year away from completing his degree and pharmacy was a stable profession in which he could support his family. The idea of playing in a premier league was appealing but the top salary was only about $1,200, nowhere near enough to tempt him.

"By then the prices had gone up and the amateurs were asking high figures," Day said in 1949. "I didn't want to turn pro because I wanted to make sure I got my final year at pharmacy. I asked them for a figure I thought they wouldn't even look at. I was the one who was surprised when they accepted. I couldn't back out then."

Hap Day signed for $5,000 and his arrival signaled the migration from amateur to pro hockey of the top-caliber players.

"It brought about an upturn in public opinion toward the pros," the *Toronto Telegram* observed in 1948, "and, as others like Day made the jump, so did the pros gain ground and the senior amateurs lose ground."

When Day signed, the NHL had two teams in Montreal as well as clubs in Ottawa, Hamilton and Toronto. The team had recently changed its name from the Toronto Blue Shirts to the Toronto St. Patricks. Day played both left wing and defense in his first game, December 15, 1924, but his debut was inauspicious.

He tripped coming off the bench on his first shift and ended up on the seat of his pants.

Things got better. Day was placed on a line with Jack Adams, the Detroit Red Wings' future managerial kingpin, at center and explosive winger Babe Dye. Both players, in radically different ways, had an impact on Day's life.

While Day toiled with the St. Patricks, Smythe was busy winning and losing the general manager's job with a new entry to the league, the New York Rangers. Smythe, a well-known figure in hockey circles with extensive connections to the amateur teams, had been hired to beat the bushes for the Rangers and he did a superb job. But when Smythe refused to acquire Dye, a performer he considered a poor team player, he fell out with Rangers' owner Colonel John Hammond and was fired before the team played a game. Smythe's work had been invaluable. In their second season, the Rangers won the Stanley Cup.

Smythe returned home and in February, 1927, pieced together the $200,000 needed to buy the St. Patricks before they were to be bought and moved by Philadelphia investors. The only on-ice assets Smythe was interested in keeping were Day and slick forward Ace Bailey. Smythe's first move was to change the name of the team to the Maple Leafs, a gesture that reflected Smythe's keen patriotism. His second decision was to move Day to defense. Day never played forward again.

Smythe installed Day as his captain in time for the club's first full season as the Maple Leafs. Ostensibly the choice of captain was democratic, but the players knew better.

"The players voted on it," Day said in 1980, "but they didn't put anybody there that Mr. Smythe didn't want."

"It was really just a formality," Ace Bailey told the *Globe and Mail* in 1990. "Hap always won. We didn't want anybody else."

Day was an excellent player. He may at times have been overshadowed by partner King Clancy, who arrived in Toronto midway through Day's tenure, but only the Rangers' Ching Johnson was considered a better defensive rearguard. As a stick checker he had no equal. Fellow players considered him the third best offensive defenseman of the era, behind Clancy and Boston's Eddie Shore.

"I figure I was a pretty good defenseman, better than some players who received far more space in the papers," Day told a writer in 1945. "But it was never natural for me to do things spectacularly so I never tried."

"He was a good defenseman, very solid, and he could hit," said Hall of Famer Clint Smith. "He wasn't a big bodychecker but he was a very intelligent player."

Day's 82 goals and 202 points were excellent offensive totals for a defenseman of his era, and he was considered a consistently dangerous scoring threat. His real gift, however, was defense.

"There's a few rules that aren't given credit to anybody but Hap Day has one," said Smith. "For instance, you can't have a hockey glove without a palm in it anymore. Hap Day was the first guy who cut the palm out of his hand. That's why we used to call him Mr. Clutch. If you were going by, he just stuck his arm out and he had you by the sweater and you couldn't get by."

The tactics amused Smythe. "Some other teams didn't like him being such a heavy lover, on the ice," Smythe wrote in his autobiography, *If You Can't Beat 'Em in the Alley.* "He'd have those arms around a guy and never let go."

Smythe knew what he had and took measures to make sure Day stuck around. He hired him at his sand and gravel pit and talked Day into buying 16 percent of the business.

"I wanted him with me summer as well as winter for a long time, which turned out to be one of my best decisions," Smythe wrote. "He was one of the best men I ever met."

Despite these sentiments, their relationship was always complicated and frequently volatile. The dynamic was never clearer than November 19, 1929. That night, Day scored four goals against Pittsburgh and sailed in on a breakaway looking for five.

"I was feeling pretty good with those four goals," Day recalled. "Anyway, I went down and had the goalkeeper beat and I missed. When I got back to the bench, he was giving me heck. And here I had already scored four goals."

The four goals remained a record for any Maple Leafs' defenseman until Ian Turnbull scored five in February, 1977. Five goals is the current league standard.

In his younger years, Day was an energetic, vital man with supreme confidence in his athleticism. "Day appeared upon the scene in his usual form," the *Telegram*'s Bob Hesketh once penned, "that is to say, walking faster than Caledon Beau can run, with his fedora tipped recklessly back on his forehead."

He once raced Hesketh from Madison Square Garden to their hotel. Day climbed into a cab stuck in gridlocked Manhattan traffic and breezed through the other door. He was also an accomplished joker. For a $12.50 bet with Charlie Conacher and Clancy, he jumped off a diving board fully clothed (including a club bag and overcoat) into a pool. He loved to cut players' ties as they slept and once snuck away from a party to tie every player's sheets into knots. The only player not at the event, Joe Primeau, was instantly blamed and, to Day's delight, doused with a fire hose while he slept.

To keep Day happy, Smythe agreed to let him run a pharmacy out of the Gardens. The business, Happy Day's Pharmacy, operated on the Carlton Street side of the Gardens, 50 feet past the west side entrance. It sold more hamburgers and milkshakes than pills before closing down after four years.

At 36, Day retired as captain but Smythe encouraged him to play one more season, with a raise, for the New York Americans. The Leafs acquired handy defenseman Wally Stanowski in return. When Day was elected to the Hockey Hall of Fame in 1961, it was as a player.

Day wasn't ready to retire to pharmacy after ending his career as a player. He read the rule book religiously and spent two years as an NHL referee before coaching a few junior teams in Toronto. Then came the Second World War, an event that catapulted Day into a new chapter with the Leafs.

Smythe was lobbying furiously to be accepted back into the service, but he had a problem behind the bench. He didn't think his coach, Dick Irvin, was tough enough to coach the Maple Leafs without Smythe pulling strings in the background.

He wanted Day.

"Hap was everything I wanted," Smythe wrote later. "He could do things I couldn't: fire people, bench them, live always on what a man could do today, not what he had done a few years ago."

When he heard that the Montreal Canadiens were looking around for a coach, Smythe suggested they hire his incumbent.

It was a move that paid off for both sides. Irvin coached the Canadiens from 1940–41 to 1954–55 and won three Cups. Day would win five.

The practical joker had matured into a rigid taskmaster. "He could be tough, he could be mean, sarcastic," said Howie Meeker. "But if at the end of the game your underwear was soaking wet, win or lose, you had no problems. If your underwear wasn't wet, you did."

Day's gift was teaching defense. "Two goals should get you a win," Day liked to say. "For one goal, you might have to settle for a tie."

"Hap Day was the best coach I ever saw operate," said Ted Kennedy. "There were other coaches very strong in certain areas but from the overall picture of knowledge of the game, knowledge of systems that must be employed to win a championship, being able to motivate players, small techniques that were vital, he was the best. We won five championships basically because of our coaching."

None was sweeter than the first, accomplished in 1941–42. In the final, the Maple Leafs trailed Jack Adams' Red Wings three games to none when Day, desperate for results, juggled his lineup. He benched Bucko McDonald and Gordie Drillon in favor of Don Metz and Gaye Stewart. Metz, playing with Syl Apps, scored four goals in the final four games.

"Drillon wasn't playing well and McDonald was physically finished in that series," Day later recalled. "I don't know if the guys we moved in made the difference but the whole team picked up."

The moves were considered key but Day said, "You didn't have to be a genius to figure something had to be done when you were down three-zero."

As important as the change in personnel was the rethinking of strategy. Over the first three games, the Red Wings had dumped the puck in and hammered the Leafs' defensemen. The dump and chase wasn't any more attractive then than it is now, and Smythe, on principle, forbade Day to use the same tactic. But a 3–0 deficit put Smythe's sense of aesthetics in perspective and he gave permission to retaliate.

The Leafs won the next three games of the series, evening it with a 3–0 shutout by Turk Broda in Detroit. The Leafs trailed 1–0 after two periods in game seven but Sweeney Schriner, Pete Langelle and then Schriner again scored, and Toronto won 3–1. It was a memorable series, symbolized by an incident after game seven in which Adams, incensed over the officiating, ran onto the ice and hit the referee.

What Hap Day orchestrated has never been repeated in the Stanley Cup finals. It would be 33 years before the trick was turned again during the post-season, when the Islanders roared back from three straight losses to defeat Pittsburgh in the 1975 Stanley Cup quarter-finals.

It wasn't akin to the present rush by championship players to endorse products, but Day did pocket some promotional money from the victory. A few days after the win, a "letter" Day had written to a pharmaceutical company was reprinted in the Toronto papers. The letter thanked the makers of Eno for keeping the team in fighting trim. Eno, the company reminded, "keeps the system free of the poisonous wastes that bring on constipation, headaches, indigestion and that listless out-of-sorts feeling."

Day's coaching style never changed over the years. Whenever the Leafs acquired a new player, Day gave his tutorial on defensive hockey. Howie Meeker recalls arriving from the army in 1946, three years removed from his last game of Junior B hockey in Stratford.

"In three weeks, he taught me how to play the game without the puck," Meeker recalled. "When you would come off the ice, he would say this is how the play developed, you did this and, if you keep doing this, you're going to get scored on. He taught me how to play the game and gave me the chance to do it."

Day would also go to the wall for a talented player. Early in the 1942–43 season, the Leafs acquired bon vivant Babe Pratt, largely on Day's assurances that he could keep the nocturnal Pratt in check. Pratt arrived in Toronto to find his roommate, both on the train and in the hotel, was his coach.

"I'm counting on you this season," Day once said to Pratt.

"Count ahead, Coach," Pratt answered, "and when you reach seven grand, I'm listening."

Pratt delivered some of the best years of his career and, in 1945, scored a Stanley Cup–winning goal when the Leafs rebounded from a mediocre regular season to upset the heavily favored Canadiens in the first round. All four victories were by one goal and the Leafs added three more one-goal wins in defeating Detroit in a seven-game final.

"No coach but Hap Day could have got us into those finals," Pratt said later.

Those one-goal victories were created in practice. Day was an early proponent of short, quick-paced workouts. The Leafs were always well-schooled in the basics that win games and championships.

His knowledge of the rules and his experience as a referee won him the respect of officials. Day would often tutor a young referee on trains or in hotel lobbies, and he was a powerful figure on the NHL's rules committee. "If Day argues a call," longtime official Bill Chadwick once said, "you have to wonder if you were wrong."

When Clancy, his old defense mate, traded in his uniform for a striped shirt, Day sent him a gift. "Here is a rule book," said the enclosed note. "Read it."

The Leafs reeled off three Cups in a row in 1947, 1948 and

1949, thanks to a brilliant team that included Jim Thomson, Bill Barilko, Wally Stanowski, Gus Mortson, Syl Apps, Bill Ezinicki, Harry Watson, Nick Metz, Howie Meeker, Ted Kennedy, Max Bentley and Turk Broda.

Day was probably the only person in the organization who could survive Smythe's meddling. Smythe had a telephone installed on the bench to relay instructions from his seat, but Day would ignore it and even leave it off the hook.

Although Smythe brooked little dissent, Day had long since proven his worth. When Smythe was in the army, Day warned him of an imminent takeover attempt by some of the club's directors. When Smythe returned home with a shrapnel injury, Day helped him organize the outright purchase of the club. Loyalty was Smythe's acid test. Incumbent general manager Frank Selke failed by remaining neutral during the takeover machinations. Day passed with flying colors.

In the spring of 1950, Smythe decided to cut back on his work. Internal injuries sustained during the war had undermined his health. The logical move was to shift Day into the general manager's role, although Day's official title was assistant GM. This move would also accommodate Joe Primeau, whom Smythe felt had solid coaching potential. Just as important, it would ensure that Day, whom Smythe trusted implicitly, would manage the team.

Primeau did, in fact, win a Stanley Cup in 1951 on Bill Barilko's overtime winner, but the Leafs were entering a lean period in which they would be shut out of the final for seven years.

Moving Day upstairs had been a cataclysmic mistake. First, the combination of Selke acquiring talent and Day polishing it had been junked, and second, for Day anything but a coaching job was a mistake. While Smythe, now in his late fifties, still had the final say on acquiring players, the team was no longer

Smythe's singular passion. He had acquired a successful racing stable and charity work was increasingly drawing away his interest. Smythe fumbled his handoff of the Maple Leafs by remaining too involved to be ignored but too distracted to be effective.

"I was the worst manager because I didn't manage," Day once said. "I worked for Smythe."

Throughout the 1950s, Harold Ballard was running the Toronto Marlboros with Stafford Smythe and trying to figure out how to gain a piece of the Maple Leafs. Gaining the old man's favor was impossible—Conn Smythe loathed Ballard.

Instead, Ballard began cultivating Hap Day. Soon, Day's game day drive invariably included a stop to pick up Ballard. Ballard flattered Day with constant questions about tactics, and the Ballards and Days visited frequently.

Hap Day had a use for Ballard as well. Stafford, who would one day own the Leafs, considered the team's brand of defensive hockey outdated. He saw Day as an obstacle to running the Maple Leafs, but perhaps Ballard could be counted on to intercede.

"Stafford said to me that he would never be involved with the Leafs as long as Hap was there," Milt Dunnell recalled. "Not that he had anything against Hap but he felt Hap would always be number one above him."

An impasse loomed. Day, despite Smythe's affection for him, would have to go to make room for another generation of Smythes.

Smythe's bluntness was a trademark, but he could not bring himself to fire his most loyal foot soldier. "I think the great regret of his hockey life was that he had to let Hap go," Dunnell said.

So Smythe used more devious tactics. In the spring of 1957, he chose a neutral site—the league's annual screening of its

Stanley Cup final promotional movie—and scripted his remarks carefully. When asked if Day would be back, Smythe said he would be "if he was available."

Day understood what was actually being said. He knew his availability had never been questioned before. "I was publicly dismembered," Day would later say. "I felt like I was walking the plank."

That day, Smythe and Dunnell shared a cab to the racetrack.

"He said, 'I suppose when we get home, I'll find out that the media has fired my general manager,'" Dunnell recalled. "I said, 'Look, I don't want any misunderstanding between us. I can tell you what our instructions to our hockey writer are. Our assessment of what happened is that Day is through.'" I thought he was going to explode. He looked at me for a few seconds and said, 'Well, you always were pretty good at sizing these things up.'"

Day eventually recovered from any initial hurt he might have felt. "I was so glad to get out, I would have dug ditches," he later said. That mild criticism was as stinging as anything Hap Day ever uttered about his time with the Leafs. "There was no wound when we parted," he once told a writer, "so there is nothing to heal."

In November, 1961, Conn Smythe finally sold his stock in the Maple Leafs and the Gardens to Stafford but was shocked to learn that his son had in turn sold a third of the shares each to John Bassett and Ballard. Ruin and disgrace followed when both Stafford and Ballard were caught siphoning money away from the Marlboros to pay for home improvements.

The ordeal destroyed Stafford who suffered a major ulcer attack. Doctors removed much of his stomach but he still suffered a massive hemorrhage of the esophagus. The idea of going to jail was more than he could bear. "See, Dad," he told his father in hospital, "I told you I won't go to jail."

A week after he entered the hospital, on October 13, 1971, Stafford Smythe died. Previously, Ballard and Smythe had bought Bassett's shares. When Ballard exercised a standing agreement to buy Smythe's shares, he gained control of the Gardens.

Day, meanwhile, spurned all overtures to return to hockey. Jack Kent Cooke, the owner of the expansion Los Angeles Kings wooed him and asked him to become the club's first coach and general manager. Day turned the offer down, along with the presidency of the American Hockey League.

Long after he retired from hockey, Hap Day's imprint was still felt. In 1969, harried Leafs' coach John McLellan said, "The next guy who tells me what Hap Day would have done with this team is going to get his brains knocked out."

Day bought a longstanding business in St. Thomas, Ontario, that manufactured wooden handles for axes, picks and shovels. He came to the business when he was 56 but worked as relentlessly as always. He would be in the plant by 5 a.m., and 12- and 14-hour workdays were the norm.

"He was a taskmaster, no question," recalled Kerry Day. "I quit on him three times but each time my mother talked some sense into me."

Day worked until he was 77 and sold the business to Kerry in 1978. Margaret, his wife, was in ill health and Day wanted to be with her every day. She died that same year.

Day's last public appearance was to perform the ceremonial face-off in the opening night of the Leafs' 1988–89 season. In 1990, it was clear that his life was nearing its end. His twin sisters, Audrey and Norma, had died a few months earlier, and he had lost a beloved granddaughter in an automobile accident. His second marriage was coming apart.

Kerry was overseas in January and part of February, 1990. When he returned, he found his father had paid his taxes in advance and cleared up all financial questions. On February 17, three days after his son had gotten home, Hap Day died in his sleep.

Kerry Day sold the company and retired comfortably. Hap Day had done it. He had supported both the family he was born into and the one he had raised himself. He had prospered as the loyal lieutenant in a family business and then built up one of his own.

The Maple Leafs wore black armbands and observed a moment of silence before their February 25, 1990, game against the New Jersey Devils. They lost 7–3. The Hap Day era had passed. Three goals didn't guarantee victory any more.

CHAPTER 2

SYL APPS

CAPTAIN, 1940–1943, 1945–48

Syl Apps lives on the thirteenth floor of his Kingston condominium where, despite the effects of a neurological illness, he occasionally receives visitors from among scores of old friends. It is wrenchingly ironic that the most athletic of all Maple Leafs lives inside an increasingly ineffective body while his mind remains as sharp as ever.

Apps, the prototypical Leafs' captain, turned 80 on January 18, 1995. He suffers from an advancing neurological disorder that first attacked his ability to walk and then to speak. The disease has continued unabated for 15 years. His doctors have never been able to establish what the illness is, and no treatment is available. Apps tires easily and four nurses attend to his care around the clock. He has not appeared in public in almost a decade but he needs only minimal medication. He communicates by pointing to a board with words and short phrases.

"It is like being prisoner in your own body," said his daughter Joanne Flint. "To not be able to walk or talk...one without the other is bearable but this is difficult."

Still, Apps follows the stock market, and the local and

national news. "He knows exactly what stocks sell for what, what's due when and for what interest," Flint said. Then she gives a reminder of the family's pride in Syl Apps. "This is a man, remember, who went on and did other great things after hockey."

Before and after hockey. Apps sat as the provincial sports commissioner during his playing days. After his great athletic career ended, he served a three-term stint as a Progressive Conservative member of provincial parliament for Kingston and the Islands and became the minister of corrections.

Syl Apps was the most glorious captain the Maple Leafs have ever had, the Olympian whose conversion to the then-disreputable world of professional sports added luster to his legend. The Leafs' third captain was a pole-vaulter at the 1936 Berlin Olympics, the Hitler Olympics, and an Empire Games champ, a sensational football player, an NHL rookie of the year and the only first-team all-star center in the Leafs' history. He is the only person inducted into the Hockey Hall of Fame, the Canadian Sports Hall of Fame, and the Canadian Amateur Athletics Hall of Fame.

Long before the clean-living Christian athlete became a cliché and often a public relations fabrication, there was Syl Apps. He did not drink, smoke or swear, and he helped turn professional athletes into true professionals.

Apps has generated more mystique than all of the captains who have followed him. Hap Day was admired but not loved by his teammates; Ted Kennedy and George Armstrong evoked loyalty and affection; Wendel Clark was trusted like a big brother; Doug Gilmour inspires with the fervor of his play. But only Syl Apps prompted awe.

"He was as fine a man as has ever lived. There wasn't anybody cut from the same cloth as Syl Apps," said Kennedy. "Besides being a great player, he was as good a man as there was off the ice. He set a standard in a career that anyone would do well to follow."

"He was the most wonderful man who ever left this town," said Fred Bemrose, a childhood friend of Apps from Paris, Ontario. "Nobody, in my estimation, came close to being the kind of man he turned out to be."

Apps was a first-team all-star in 1938–39 and 1941–42 and a second-team all-star three other times. He finished his ten-year career with 56 penalty minutes, averaging less than three minor penalties a season.

But the most lasting legacy of Apps' captaincy is the banners that hang from the rafters of Maple Leaf Gardens. Syl Apps was a winner. In the six years he was captain, the Leafs won three Stanley Cups including two in his final two seasons. The Leafs made the playoffs nine times in his ten years. Nice guys don't always finish last.

In a sense, Syl Apps is no longer of this time. Athletic shoe commercials, capricious agents and spiraling salaries have made this age the age of the sporting anti-hero. Although hockey remains the least affected of the major sports, it was tarnished, perhaps forever, by the 1994 owner-imposed lock-out. Players such as Craig Janney have refused to report to Canadian teams for fear of depreciating their lucrative U.S. dollar incomes. Others violate legally binding contracts as easily as they hold an opponent's stick.

Syl Apps, who in 1943 tried to return $1,000 of his $6,000 salary to Conn Smythe because he had missed half the season with a broken leg, watches these events on television. He is saddened by the games lost to the lockout but unshaken in his belief that athletes should strive to be role models. He is without rancor. When asked about the athletes of today, he points to his board to say he has no comment. His response should come, his daughter said, as no surprise. "I have never heard my father speak in less than the most complimentary of terms," said Flint, "of anybody who is not in the room with him."

While Apps has always considered what he was doing that day to be the most important part of his life, hindsight and memory have deepened his appreciation for his time as a hockey player. When asked how he would like to be remembered, Syl Apps, politician, Olympian and professional sports star, says: "As a pretty good hockey player."

Charles Joseph Sylvanus Apps was born January 18, 1915, in Paris, Ontario.

His parents, Mary Wrigley and Ernest Apps, lived in the north end of the city, the prosperous end, at 36 Banfield Street. The Apps were already well established by the time Syl, the middle of three children, arrived. Ernest Apps' father had built the Apps Mill, now a conservation area and historic site. An Apps window gleams in the Paris Baptist Church. Apps' contact with his hometown remains strong. He still subscribes to the weekly newspaper, the *Paris Star*.

The family was upper middle class. Ernest Apps operated a drug store in town with his brother, Thomas, an optometrist. Mary was related to the American Wrigley family, owners of the Chicago Cubs and the chewing gum company.

It was a strict Baptist household with no alcohol kept in the house. "Dad grew up in the same sort of home we grew up in," said Joanne. "Nothing was given, everything was earned."

Apps learned to skate when his father, an athletic man who excelled in baseball, began flooding an indentation at the rear of the property. Later, Ernest Apps made a rink in an alley and nailed trash can lids to the garage door for his son to practice shooting at.

Despite the ravages of the Depression, Apps has never mentioned hardship or privation. He told an interviewer in 1983, "We had more fun in the small towns than kids do today. There weren't as many distractions. I can remember in Paris, all we would do all summer long was play different sports."

Apps shone in every sport he tried. He was an excellent ballplayer and a southwestern Ontario tennis champion. He was good at golf and a gifted track and field competitor. At 14, Apps played junior hockey against players who were sometimes six years older. He was the youngest junior player in the Ontario Hockey Association.

Even then, a star quality clung to him. "Everybody liked him," said Bemrose. "A lot of us kids felt he was something special, even in those days."

In 1931, Ernest Apps became ill while tending his shop during the winter. His condition weakened and, finally, at Christmastime, he died of pneumonia.

"Everyone felt so bad for that family," Bemrose recalled. "You'd see Syl walking home from school and your heart would go out to him."

Syl played three years of intermediate hockey before graduating from Paris High School at 16, a year after his father's death, as the valedictorian. McMaster University in Hamilton was the obvious choice for Apps; it was a Baptist school not too far away from home, and Apps studied political science and economics. At McMaster, Syl met Mary Josephine Marshall (known to everyone as Molly Jo) and the two began a courtship.

Apps' athletic ability was by now too impressive to ignore. For no particular reason, he picked up the pole vault. "I was always interested in it," Apps said. He won the pole vaulting championships at the British Empire Games in London in 1934 and two years later represented Canada at the Olympics, the games in which Jesse Owens flew in the face of Adolph

Hitler. Apps finished sixth and saw Hitler. "Unfortunately, I was too young to pay too much attention to what was going on around me," he said.

Apps downplayed his Olympic appearance in later years. "In those days, there wasn't as much attention on the athletes as there is now," Apps said. "It just didn't mean that much."

The circumstances surrounding Apps' arrival in Toronto have long since passed into legend. Apps came to Conn Smythe's attention in 1934 when one of his cronies, Bill Marsden, saw Apps playing hockey at McMaster. Smythe is said to have chuckled dismissively when he heard that the player's name was Sylvanus Apps. "No one with a name like that could possibly become a pro hockey player," Smythe is reported to have said.

Nevertheless, while watching the McMaster halfback steamroll over the University of Toronto Blues in a football game at Varsity Stadium, Smythe became so convinced he had a prospect that he left the game at halftime to wire the NHL and put Apps on the Leafs' protected list.

"Any guy who plays football the way this guy plays must be good at my game too," said Smythe.

It took all of Smythe's considerable powers of salesmanship to convince the Apps family that playing for the Maple Leafs was worthwhile. Smythe visited Mary Apps repeatedly, apprising her of the money her son could earn and send home should he sign with the Leafs. Still, Syl Apps remained on the protected list for two years before deciding on the ship home from the Berlin Olympics to join the club.

What would be a coveted offer today held only lukewarm appeal for Apps in 1936. The pro game was still locked in a struggle with senior hockey for the attention of fans, and the Allan Cup had as much as or more prestige than the Stanley Cup. Radio would soon convert players into household names, but the only way for most Canadians to watch hockey was to go to the local rink. Hometown loyalty continued largely unabated until the advent of television.

Hockey was generally played by poorly educated, rough men and gambling was such an accepted part of the spectacle that Conn Smythe reserved a special section high behind the grays in which gamblers operated. Educated men rarely considered careers as hockey players because most professions paid as much or more and promised a much longer working life.

Apps knew he was good enough to play in the NHL. The year before, as a temporary member of the Maple Leafs, he had more than held his own in a small barnstorming series that saw Toronto and the Chicago Blackhawks play three games in Vancouver. It was the hockey player's lack of standing and prestige that troubled Apps and his family.

"Actually, in my circle, professional athletes were not looked upon as the right sort," he later told a writer. "However, I discussed the situation with Molly Marshall, she was my girl, and, because jobs were scarce, she agreed it was a golden opportunity, but I was still afraid what her parents would think. However, I signed with the Leafs and was I ever relieved when her parents welcomed me back."

Although he had played only a hundred games as an amateur, Apps was an instant sensation when he hit the NHL.

"He came to the Leafs as an Olympic athlete from McMaster University and he had all the attributes of the purist," said Milt Dunnell. "He never drank or smoked or swore and he was probably the cleanest hockey player anyone had seen. All those things went into it."

Playing on a line with Gordie Drillon and Harvey Jackson, the 21-year-old Apps made a strong impression among the rookies.

"It was thought he might display nervousness, but instead he acted like an old-timer. Some of his passes were beauties and he played his position to the king's taste," wrote the *Toronto Evening Telegram* after the 1936–37 season opener.

That season, Apps won the inaugural Calder Trophy for rookie of the year, collecting 79 out of a possible 81 points while leading the league in assists.

And if Apps wasn't the best player in the NHL, he may have been the most graceful. He possessed a fluid, athletic skating stroke and loved to pick up the puck in his own end for rink-long dashes. He passed the puck intuitively.

His moral convictions shone through even on the ice. Apps is known to have breathed an oath only once and he disliked fighting. Word got around the league about a rookie who wouldn't fight, but when Boston's Flash Hollett accidentally high-sticked Apps and knocked out two teeth, Apps charged Hollett and won a clear decision. It was one of only three fights in his career. He fought Chicago defenseman Joe Cooper when Cooper speared him in the ribs and battled Detroit tough guy Jim Orlando in a Toronto-Detroit brawl.

The rookie later centered the remnants of the Kid Line, skating between Busher Jackson and Charlie Conacher. In his third season, Apps moved between right-winger Gordie Drillon and Bob Davidson on the left side to form the DAD line. Davidson was the checker while Apps and Drillon were dominant offensive talents.

In 1941–42, Apps earned no penalties and won the Lady Byng Trophy as the most gentlemanly and sportsmanlike player in the league. The post-season brought the highlight of his career when the Leafs lost the first three games of the Stanley Cup final to Detroit and came back to win four in a row and their second championship. Apps picked up no points in the first three losses, but in game four Hap Day benched Drillon, juggled the lineup and inserted Don Metz on Apps' left side. In that game, Apps scored the tying goal and set up the winner. He finished the series with seven points, including three goals over the final four games. He calls that cup his most satisfying moment in hockey.

By now, his athleticism was winning widespread admiration. "He's a Rembrandt on the ice, a Nijinsky at the goal-mouth," gushed *Sport*. "He plays with such grace and precision, you get the impression that every move is the execution of a mental image conceived long before he goes through the motions."

Detroit Red Wings' general manager Jack Adams called Apps "the greatest center I have ever seen."

"His stickhandling and his speed made him special. He didn't go out knocking anybody down too much but he would check them," said longtime linemate Bob Davidson. "He wouldn't deliberately go out and hurt a guy but he played to win all the time."

Apps charged the net hard and his style took a rigorous toll on his body. He tore shoulder muscles in 1938–39, broke his collarbone the following season and injured his knee in 1940–41. Aside from his rookie year, he never played a season without losing games to injuries.

In 1940, Apps succeeded Red Horner as the Leafs' captain in one of the most remarkable changeovers in league history. Horner had long symbolized the Leafs' pugnacious attitude. In the wild 1930s, he led the league in penalty minutes for eight consecutive seasons. Apps' career penalty total was far lower than Horner's total in any one season.

But after two seasons as captain, Apps volunteered for the armed forces and Bob Davidson, a gritty and conscientious player, assumed the C.

By now, the Apps had three children but Syl was accepted

into the army and immediately volunteered for the Pacific theater. He was commissioned as a lieutenant and finished at the top of his class of 80 officer cadets, earning one of the highest ratings ever.

When he returned in 1945, the captaincy was waiting.

During the year, the Leafs had acquired Harry Watson, a talented left-winger who Smythe was convinced would make an excellent defenseman. "It lasted about one practice," Watson recalled. "Syl came down, deked me out of my jockstrap and scored. The next practice, I was on his left."

Apps didn't miss a beat upon his return. He was immediately reinstated as captain and paired with the rambunctious Wild Bill Ezinicki on his right side. In his comeback season, Apps recorded 24 goals, up to then a career high.

Ezinicki was an unwitting participant in the only incident in which anyone could remember hearing Syl Apps swear. In a game against Detroit, Ezinicki took aim at Gordie Howe but accidentally hammered Apps. "Somebody said he never swore," recalled Howe. "I know one time I stepped out of the way and Ezinicki hit him and I heard some words I've never heard before."

It was the only known breach in his career. The *Toronto Star* called Apps "the apostle of clean living," and Smythe, who envisioned a Maple Leaf Gardens created as much for the elites as for the masses, was entranced. He loved to brag about "my teetotaling captain" and gave the family a choice of the best seats at the Gardens. Molly chose seats in the northeast corner, near what would later become Harold Ballard's bunker. The family still holds these tickets.

Along with his playing duties, Apps coached the Upper Canada College varsity hockey team. He was a regular after-dinner speaker for boy scout troops and church groups. While Molly occasionally took a social drink, Apps never did.

"I know it [liquor] won't do me any good but it might do me some harm," he once said to Army buddy Ted Collins.

But Apps did not wear his piety on his sleeve. He was a well-liked as well as a well-respected captain.

"He was still one of the boys," said Watson. "He and Molly would go to house parties. Syl wouldn't drink but Molly would have one or two. All of a sudden, you'd look up and they were gone."

As the team's designated leader, Apps prided himself on being a team player. One year, he was in a race for the scoring title, with $1,000 going to the winner. Apps and Jimmy Thomson were each credited with an assist on a Watson goal. As soon as the game ended, Apps went to the scorer and told him his assist should go to Ezinicki.

"The success of the Leafs of those days was that they had a wonderful team, not just a collection of individual players," said Rangers' Hall of Famer Edgar Laprade. "I don't think Syl would stand out like Gordie Howe or someone of that nature but he was always there and you could always depend on him."

Apps scored the overtime winner in game four of the 1947 final against Montreal and added two more in the Leafs' 1948 Stanley Cup championship run, but the appeal of the game was leaving him. The last benchmark he wanted to hit before retiring was 200 goals. Smythe believed Apps had several good years left and, while Apps was certain to leave too soon to suit Smythe, at least he might get another year. So Smythe was not unhappy when Apps was stuck at 198 goals with only one regular season game left in the 1947–48 schedule.

But Apps netted his fifth and final hat trick in Detroit on March 28, 1948, to finish his career with 201 goals. He followed through with his retirement plans even though his 26-goal and 53-point season were career highs. Apps was a finalist for both the Hart and the Lady Byng Trophies and Smythe, convinced he could play several more years, offered him a blank contract. Apps never returned it.

"The decision that I made to leave hockey wasn't because I didn't think I was capable of it," he told the *Toronto Star* in 1983. "It was because I wondered what I was doing with myself. I remember being in Chicago, lying around on a Sunday afternoon waiting for a game and I just thought, 'What am I doing here? I have a wife and kids at home that I don't see very much. This is sort of stupid. Maybe it's time I forgot about it.'"

Apps was 33 and the reigning captain when he retired. Despite forfeiting two years to the army, he finished as a point-a-game player—432 points in 423 games. Only two players who have been Leafs for more than three seasons, Darryl Sittler and Rick Vaive, have averaged a point a game or more. Sittler averaged 1.08 points a game, Apps 1.02 and Vaive one point per game. In today's higher scoring world, Doug Gilmour and Dave Andreychuk are on pace to eclipse these marks easily and Ed Olczyk, who played three seasons with the Maple Leafs, averaged 1.03 points per game.

Apps already had one foot in the non-hockey world when he retired. In his final season, the governing provincial Tories had appointed him provincial athletic commissioner.

In 1949, this father of four was named Canadian father of the year. Naturally enough, he donated the $100 prize to charity.

Apps' post-Maple Leafs career was richly varied and successful. He briefly coached the Toronto Marlboros, did some television commentary, commuted to the University of Western Ontario to upgrade his education and worked as a sporting goods supervisor for Simpson-Sears. After eight years, he became president of Milton Brick and, in 1963, bought his own firm, Dunbrick, in Kingston.

Apps had always been interested in politics. While still a

player, he had unsuccessfully sought the federal seat for Brant but lost by fewer than 200 votes.

One day he learned in a conversation with several friends that the provincial Tories needed a candidate for Kingston and the Islands. Apps ran and in 1963 won the first of three terms. He prospered as a widely respected if unobtrusive back-bencher. After he chaired a select committee on youth for two years, the plight of young people became one of his abiding passions. In February, 1971, wearing a tie his eight-year-old granddaughter Mary had sewn for him, Apps nominated Bill Davis for the Conservative Party's leadership. When Davis succeeded John Robarts as premier, Apps was named minister of corrections.

MPPs liked him because, regardless of party affiliation, he followed up inquiries about young people in the justice system. "With no fanfare Syl Apps has eliminated most of the abuses and has earned the respect of prisoners, staff and opposition critics," NDP opposition critic Morton Shulman said on Apps' retirement from the House in 1974.

There was heartbreak to come. Molly died of cancer in the spring of 1982 and Apps' sister Yvonne died a week later. While he was left disconsolate by these losses, Apps continued to work.

He spoke little in the House. He opposed liberalizing liquor laws but showed a progressive streak during his tenure as minister of corrections. "Personally, I know a lot of young people with beards and long hair who are just as normal as everybody else," Apps said in *Hansard*.

Apps' athletic legacy continued. His son Bob played for the B.C. Lions of the Canadian Football League, and Syl Apps Jr. played ten NHL seasons for the New York Rangers, Pittsburgh and Los Angeles.

Through the years, Syl Apps' character has remained

unchanged. He was presented with a gold token, good for life-time admission to any event at the Gardens, but he has never removed the gift from its box.

"He's not one to go through life on privilege," said Joanne Flint. "He wants to pay his own way."

Writer Arnold Irish described Apps as "pleasant and alto-gether cooperative to be sure, a likable man who gives polite, precise answers to questions, but who rarely expatiates. A seri-ous man who doesn't take himself too seriously."

In public life as an Olympic athlete, Toronto Maple Leaf and politician, Syl Apps viewed controversy as if it were a brother vice to tobacco, alcohol and lawlessness.

Apps, a devout and clean-living man, was a perfect role model for a serious city.

"He was convinced," former NDP leader Stephen Lewis once said of Apps, "that the way to get a boy out of trouble was to get him into a hockey league sponsored by a church. And I rather think that's been Syl through all of his government career."

Apps was, and is, a true conservative; the indomitability of the individual and the virtues of hard work lie at the heart of his beliefs.

"My father taught us never to be in awe of anyone," Flint said. "Respect people, but never be in awe of them. He is ideo-logically and in practice a conservative."

Through Flint provincial officials have approached Apps to take a role in information campaigns publicizing programs and technological improvements for people with disabilities. It is yet another role, Flint says, that her father can grow into. Apps' mother lived until 93, he remains fit and strong, and his passion for leadership has not been extinguished.

"He's always been a role model and I think what's going to happen is he's going to be a role model again, this time for disabled people," Flint said. "He's been in a bit of a trough for the last couple of years, but I think there's a huge role for him there that he will someday want to fill."

The voice has been stilled, but the spirit lives on.

"I can't talk, I can't walk, I can't write," Syl Apps says, pointing to the words on a board. "But I feel fine."

CHAPTER 3

TED KENNEDY

CAPTAIN, 1948–1955, 1956–57

T he hall is narrow, painted in dull hues. The man at the end opens the door to his Spartan office and ushers you in.

At 69, Ted Kennedy projects a military air, an aura that suits Fort Erie Race Track's chief of security and one of Conn Smythe's most beloved foot soldiers. In his office, the end one in the squat administration building that borders the racetrack, no pictures of either his family or famous past line the desk or wall. There's just a bare desk, a filing cabinet, some chairs and a large picture of Queen Elizabeth, benignly watching a still-loyal subject.

Ted Kennedy has worked here, in the shadow of the Canada-U.S. border, for ten years. He presides over a security staff that has dwindled from 40 in the heady days of the mid-1980s to 24. "The way the economy is," said Kennedy, "we have had to downsize like everyone else."

He remains an enormously vital man, active in the social life of Maple Leafs' alumni. Kennedy is perhaps 20 pounds over his rookie parlaying weight of 185 pounds but the features, layered around Irish eyes and a battered nose, remain jovial.

The man gesturing at the end of the hall could be anybody's grandfather.

Ted Kennedy was born in 1925 in Humberstone, Ontario, an hour's drive from his current workplace. The village became a part of Port Colborne in 1952. The fourth and final child in his family, he was born to a grieving mother. A month before his son's birth, Gordon Kennedy was rabbit hunting in a nearby field with a friend. He stuck his rifle into the wire fence he was climbing and jumped over. The gun either fell on the ground and went off or caught on a piece of wire that jarred the trigger. With his friend 35 yards away, it's impossible to know for sure. Gordon Kennedy crumpled to the ground, shot in the back.

The friend carried Kennedy 300 yards to his car and rushed him to Niagara Falls Hospital. The shot had torn a hole in his left side and lead pellets were lodged in his spine. Nonetheless, Kennedy's doctors were hopeful of a recovery. But two weeks later an infection set in that required an operation and the next morning, Gordon Kennedy died. He was 35.

Kennedy worked at the local grain elevator and whatever income the family had disappeared with his death. He was Margaret Kennedy's second and final husband. Her first, Tom King, had died of influenza. Tragedy would strike the family again in 1963 when Joe, Kennedy's half-brother and a vice-president with IBM Canada, died in a plane crash.

The family, like Hap Day's, succeeded because of the strength of its matriarch. For 25 years, Margaret Kennedy worked two jobs to keep the family afloat. During the day, she was the superintendent of a Bell Canada building in Port Colborne. At night, she sold hot dogs at the White Arena around the corner from her home.

"What she did wasn't that unusual," said Kennedy. "She never applied for help from anyone. She was Irish, very, very independent and very, very proud. She had to be both a mother and a father to us."

Ted's sister Jesse operated another hot dog stand in the rink and when the Kennedys weren't working in the rink, they were playing in it. White Arena was the birthplace of Ted Kennedy the hockey player.

"We played for hours there," Kennedy recalled. "In order to get on the ice free, we'd clean the ice. Then, after a hockey game, they would let us out on the ice to have a shinny game for an hour."

By his early teens, Theodore Kennedy had become Ted and then Teeder. The NHL has been home to two Gretzkys and several Marios but only one Teeder. Kennedy grinned when asked about his nickname.

"My mother always called me Theodore, but some of the people around town had trouble pronouncing it," Kennedy recalled. "They'd shout what sounded like, 'Hi, Teedore,' or 'Hello, Teedor,' and eventually it became Teeder."

A Welland newspaperman called him Teeder in a dispatch, and the nickname followed Kennedy to Toronto and beyond.

Teeder Kennedy grew up hard-working and athletic. By high school, he was excelling in football and positioning himself to play in the backfield at the University of Western Ontario where he planned to study business. Word of his hockey talent reached Montreal through bird dog Dinty Moore, and Kennedy was offered a chance to play for Montreal's junior team, the Royals.

The club offered to foot the bill for his billeting and tuition at Lower Canada College, a prestigious private school in Montreal. This arrangement pleased Margaret Kennedy, who saw a chance for Ted to acquire a more polished education. Joe, Kennedy's older half-brother, had graduated from Western's business program and she was anxious for her youngest child to follow in his footsteps. Ted, meanwhile, saw a chance to play hockey.

But administrative mistakes and a 16-year-old's homesickness undermined any future Kennedy might have enjoyed with the Canadiens. When he arrived in Montreal, Kennedy found no team official to greet him. He took a cab to the Queen's Hotel, the headquarters for both the Royals and the parent Canadiens. He could find no Royals officials there either. In fact, it took days for a Royals representative to contact him. Kennedy scrimmaged for a few days with the Canadiens but the unguided transition from Humberstone to downtown Montreal frightened him. He had never stayed in a hotel before, much less made his way in a strange city.

"A representative from the Royals took me out to Lower Canada College and enrolled me in class," Kennedy said. "I was supposed to get into a home in Westmount but in the meantime I was still being billeted at the Queen's Hotel."

Finding himself academically far behind his classmates only compounded Kennedy's unhappiness.

"Anyway, I'm still shuttling back and forth on the streetcar," Kennedy recalled. "I asked the Royals, 'When am I going to get into a home around the college?' They said they were working on it and so on. That's when I said no, I had enough."

Discouraged, homesick and absolutely convinced he was giving up any chance of playing in the NHL, Ted Kennedy packed his one suitcase. Three weeks after leaving home, he took the train back to Humberstone.

But the Canadiens still held his rights. At the end of the season, they sent a Royals representative to sign Kennedy to a captaincy form, to retain him as a Montreal prospect. Kennedy refused.

"I didn't hold anything against them but I felt they were a little negligent in not making an arrangement for me. I guess they felt I would be enamored with just being there but I wasn't. It was the exact opposite.

Back home, Kennedy became an apprentice of Nels Stewart. Stewart, who had enjoyed a glorious NHL career in the 1920s and 1930s, was coaching a team of senior players and he conscripted the 16-year-old Kennedy. Kennedy was a gifted scorer but not a natural skater. He would never break the 30-goal mark or finish higher than fifth in an NHL scoring race but Stewart taught him to make the best of the limited chances he enjoyed.

"The big thing Nels taught me was, if you had that extra bit of a second, take a look before shooting," said Kennedy. "That's something I always remembered."

Stewart's nickname, Old Poison, accurately described an on-ice nasty streak and Kennedy mirrored Stewart's toughness.

"Nels Stewart was a tremendous competitor and he had a stick that was sort of like a nine-iron," said Bob Davidson, a longtime Kennedy teammate who faced Stewart often. "He would get that stick around his opponent's eyes. He was a very determined player."

When the lessons took, Stewart referred his prodigy to Frank Selke. Selke was running the Maple Leafs while Conn Smythe was serving with his Sportsmen's Battery, a unit of writers, athletes and sporting figures he had assembled for wartime duty. The Leafs, Stanley Cup champions the year before, were staggering to a .500 season and a first-round elimination.

Kennedy grew up a Leafs' fan and wore number nine throughout his minor hockey career in tribute to Leafs' great Charlie Conacher. He wasn't willing to return to Montreal but, when Stewart offered the chance to play in Toronto, Kennedy, then finishing his Grade 11 year, jumped at it.

"My hockey season was over. I was in class one day, when

the principal of the school got me out of class and said there was a phone call from Toronto. This was about 2:30 in the afternoon and it was Nels Stewart. He said the Leafs have made a deal with the Canadiens to get me on their negotiation list and Frank Selke and Hap Day would like me to come talk with them."

This time, Stewart met Kennedy at the station and took him to the meeting with Hap Day, the Leafs' coach, and Selke. Then came the most difficult hurdle—Margaret Kennedy's permission.

"My mother was very annoyed," Kennedy said. "She wanted me to continue my schooling and go to university. Finally, she said, 'If that's what your heart is set on, you do what you like.'"

The signing would ultimately drive a wedge between Selke and the autocratic Smythe. The Canadiens still technically owned Kennedy's rights, and the Maple Leafs acquired Kennedy by trading the rights to Frank Eddolls, a highly touted junior defenseman, to Montreal. Eddolls was serving in the RCAF when he learned of the trade and Smythe, a zealous patriot, was angry on two fronts. He objected to the Maple Leafs, whose very symbol meant heritage, trading a serviceman. More importantly, he sensed a coup looming among directors eager to push him aside and place Selke, also a gifted administrator, in the general manager's chair. Smythe tried to have the deal revoked but history bears witness to Selke's brilliance. Frankie Eddolls would last eight years in the NHL, three with Montreal and five with the sad-sack New York Rangers, before fading into anonymity. Teeder Kennedy would become a star.

Selke, who called Kennedy "the greatest competitor in hockey," would not preside over Kennedy's ascent to stardom.

When Smythe, wounded by shrapnel, returned from overseas, he moved quickly to secure a majority of shares in Maple

Leaf Gardens. Selke insisted on remaining neutral during these machinations, a move Smythe interpreted as treasonous. As Smythe assembled the necessary financing to become the principal owner, it became obvious that Selke would be fired. He quit instead, went to work for the Canadiens and managed them to six Stanley Cups.

The Leafs had lost Syl Apps, among others, to the war effort and Kennedy was conscripted into the lineup for the final two games of the 1942–43 season.

"You didn't play in the NHL as a 17-year-old," said Kennedy. "In those years if you were playing, you were either too young, too old or 4-F."

Kennedy did not play in the post-season as the Maple Leafs lost to Detroit in the first round. But in his second year, he scored 26 goals and collected 49 points in as many games.

"He could do everything but skate," said Howie Meeker, who was the rookie of the year in 1946–47 after a season spent on Kennedy's right. "If he could have skated like I could, or like Vic Lynn could, there never would have been a greater center."

Kennedy fearlessly sought the puck in the corners. He was tested early and often, and, while he rarely won a fight, Kennedy never hesitated to use his stick as an equalizer.

"I remember Elmer Lach coming into a face-off and saying he was going to do something to Kennedy," Bob Davidson said. "He was trying to scare him because Kennedy was so young. Kennedy said, 'Go ahead and try.' Kennedy would have carved him."

Ted Kennedy played desperate hockey every day of his life. His work ethic, forged in poverty in Humberstone and polished by Stewart, was his greatest asset.

"With a guy like Teeder, it's born into you," said Sid Smith, a Kennedy linemate for six seasons. "It's the will to win. He wanted to be good, all the time, and he wanted you to be good too."

Hap Day was the perfect coach for Kennedy's still-emerging talents. Day preached defense and positioning, solid physical play and the importance of face-offs. None of these require great skating ability and it was on these basics that Teeder Kennedy built his game. Kennedy was more than the best face-off man of his era. He was one of the best face-off artists of any era.

Even today, the thought of Day inspires Kennedy. His manner, gentle in reminiscence, becomes passionate in recalling the coach who fashioned his career. "He drummed it into us that face-offs, particularly in our own end, were vital. If you don't do the right thing on a face-off, it could cost you a game, maybe a championship.

"Day would show you the little things, the things some coaches didn't know. My reflexes were always quite good but, again, because he stressed the importance of face-offs, every face-off, that's how I learned. It was the training. It wasn't hit and miss."

Suddenly, Kennedy is on his feet, reaching for an umbrella. His message seems urgent now. Kennedy positions himself as an opposing center and uses the umbrella to demonstrate how Day taught him to latch on to an opponent's stick and tie him up during the face-off. He sits back down. His fingers begin to snap and the cadence of his speech becomes even more forceful.

"If we won the draw, players knew where they went." Snap. "If we lost the draw, they still knew where they went." Snap. "Your defensemen were in position, this is basic hockey. He stressed it so emphatically that when we went into a face-off we knew how vital it was. Every face-off…"

And then Ted Kennedy stops talking. He is silent, intent for a minute or so. He apologizes, reminds himself to breathe and takes a drink of water. He cannot explain himself. "It just comes rushing back," is all he can say. Forty years after his retirement, the emotion is an unwelcome hangover, a leftover kernel of passion that has popped to the surface. But if it embarrasses him now, it defined him as a player.

"I think every player on our team looked up to him," said Bob Davidson. "They knew, just to look at him and see the look on his face when he went into a face-off. He was just so intense."

Kennedy respects Smythe but his reverence is reserved for Syl Apps and Hap Day. He calls Apps the greatest Maple Leaf who ever lived and regrets that Apps has had to withdraw from the public eye for health reasons, depriving a generation of fans of his name and the tales of his greatness.

But Kennedy's endorsement of Apps as the Leafs' greatest player, let alone captain, is by no means unanimous. Sid Smith, who played with both, says that, for his money, Kennedy was better.

"I thought Syl Apps was a great one too. I only played a year and a half with Syl. But if I assess both of them, I would say Teeder was best. He had more gumption. Syl was a great captain, but I don't know whether he had some of the things Teeder had, like the work ethic. Not that he was lazy, but Teeder was a better forechecker and he kept the guys on edge, working all the time."

That intensity won Kennedy a legion of admirers, including a fan named John Arnott. Several times a game, from his seat in the blues, Arnott would bellow his famous cry, "Come on, Teeder," during a lull in the action. The cry became a standard at the Gardens and, after a time, the two men met for an awkward handshake. Years after Kennedy's retirement, they met again in Nobleton, where Kennedy operated a horse farm and

Arnott had built a house. A strong friendship developed and, when John Arnott died in the early 1980s, Ted Kennedy was one of his pallbearers.

Kennedy was a key contributor to the 1945 championship in which the Leafs defeated the powerhouse Canadiens along the way. Former Maple Leafs' coach Dick Irvin called the 1944–45 Canadiens the greatest team in 20 years and he had ample evidence to back up his claim. Maurice "Rocket" Richard scored 50 goals in as many games and the Habs' vaunted Punch Line—Lach, Richard and Toe Blake—finished 1–2–3 in the scoring race. But Kennedy, Davidson and Mel Hill shut the Punch Line down as the Leafs defeated Montreal in six. Richard exploded for four goals in game five but managed only one other in the series. In game one, Kennedy scored the winner with 22 seconds left in the third period and added another in the Leafs' 3–2 victory in game two. In all, Kennedy scored four times and led the final in points as Toronto outlasted Detroit in seven games to win an unlikely Stanley Cup.

"We shouldn't have beaten them and again there was Day," remembered Kennedy. "He knew if we were going to beat the Canadiens, we would have to go with our best. In order to do that, he had to play his best troops as often as he could. We went at it with two lines, four defensemen and one centerman, Nick Metz, who was back from the service. Metz would spell off Gus Bodnar and myself and that's how we wound up beating the Canadiens in the semis."

The playoffs were Kennedy's finest hour. Never a first team all-star, never a scoring champion, Kennedy contented himself with winning. In Toronto only Dave Keon, with 32 post-season goals, and Wendel Clark, who has 31, have more playoff goals than Kennedy's 29. When Kennedy arrived, the Leafs had won three Stanley Cups in their history. When he retired at the end of the 1956–57 season, the Leafs were victors in eight.

In the 1947 six-game victory over Montreal, Kennedy was the club's leading scorer and netted the Stanley Cup winner. Syl Apps retired after that season and in the fall of 1948, 22-year-old Ted Kennedy became the club's youngest ever captain.

It was an event, Kennedy recalled, remarkably free of fanfare.

"In the dressing room one day, prior to the season starting, Hap comes in and says, 'Look, we have to have another captain. Have you fellows got anything to say?' Turk Broda spoke right up. He says, 'I think Teeder should be the captain.' It wasn't put to a vote. Day said, 'Do you have anyone else in mind?' Nobody spoke up. Then he said to me, 'Do you consent to be the captain of the club?' I said I would be honored. That's how it happened."

While he relished being captain, Kennedy remembers straining to make sure that wearing the C didn't politicize his role as player.

"There wasn't much separation between the captain and the rest of the players. Whoever the coach was, Hap Day, King Clancy, Joe Primeau, they had complete control of the team. You'd never criticize another player. If you did, you'd be shot down in a minute. That was left up to the coach."

His teammates remember a different Kennedy.

"He was what a captain should be," said Meeker. "He would coax, he would plead and, if that didn't work, he would cuss you out to get the very best you had."

"If you let your man go or did something wrong, Teeder would let you know," said Sid Smith. "You wouldn't walk out of the rink with a chip on your shoulder; you would just say your piece constructively. Teeder would do that more than most because he was the captain."

The Leafs in 1950 were gunning for their fourth consecutive Cup. In the third period of the first game of the final at the

Detroit Olympia, Kennedy and Gordie Howe were involved in the pivotal moment of the series.

"We had knocked Detroit off two or three years in a row and they were terribly upset," Kennedy recalled. "In the first game in Detroit, I get the puck at our blue line and I'm coming up the side and out of the corner of my eye, I see Howe coming at a full rate of speed. He's got me in his sights and he's got one thing on his mind—to put me into the fence. I couldn't outskate him. I was carrying the puck and I couldn't outskate him if I wasn't carrying the puck. I pulled up and he went right across in front of me and he hit his head on the boards."

"Howe went to stop but couldn't, his skates got caught or something, and he went headfirst into the boards," said Meeker, who was watching from the bench only feet away. "Nobody touched him."

"Tommy Ivan [the Wings' bantamweight coach] said I butt-ended him," Kennedy recalled. "I said, 'Tommy, I'm sorry Gordie is hurt but I had nothing to do with it. They're claiming when I pulled up my stick hit him in the face, but what happened is he tried to pull out of it, lost his balance and went into the dasher'."

Howe recalls the incident differently. He said Kennedy hit him with his stick but did so accidentally while following through with a pass a split second before the two met.

"From my analysis, he couldn't have butt-ended me because he was right-handed," Howe said. "But when he passed the puck, he came around and the stick hit me. I ate it in the eye. That's what did my nose in."

Howe had to be rushed to hospital where he needed emergency surgery to relieve the pressure on his brain. While a league investigation cleared Kennedy of any wrongdoing, the furor over the accident overshadowed the series. Kennedy, playing with a severe charley horse, was ineffective the rest of the way. It took seven games but the Red Wings, long shots with Howe injured, beat the Maple Leafs with a ferocious effort in seven intense and physical games.

"I think the whole thing had an adverse effect on the attitude of the team," Kennedy said. "I couldn't provide the leadership that might have made the difference. In spite of taking an awful lot of abuse in the press, I could deal with it. What I couldn't deal with was the charley horse."

The Leafs won the Cup in 1951 but the Detroit upset had killed the possibility of winning five in a row. Kennedy scored twice in the victory over Montreal in the final, including an overtime goal. The 1951 title would be Kennedy's fifth and final championship. Bill Barilko, who potted the Cup winner, was killed in a plane crash that summer and the Leafs began to descend into mediocrity. Kennedy's numbers began a similar slide. In 1954–55, Kennedy scored ten goals, logged 52 points and won the Hart Trophy, but it was bestowed to honor a career, not a season.

An NHL career spent squeezing superb efforts out of leaden legs had taken its toll. At 30, Ted Kennedy retired to the business world. He lasted 18 months but, after repeated pleas from Day, agreed to come back in 1956–57 to try to help the Leafs, now coached by his old linemate Howie Meeker, make the playoffs. He scored six goals in 30 games. The Maple Leafs finished fifth. It was over.

"He worked like a dog but guys that normally couldn't catch him were able to now," Meeker recalled. "He had lost that half a step."

Smythe, who considered Meeker a poor coach but a fine theorist, disagreed. He believed Kennedy had several years left in him. This time, though, Kennedy could not be dissuaded from retiring permanently.

He coached the Peterborough Petes for a season. A young

coach named Scotty Bowman watched Kennedy tutor his young charges on face-offs, and uses the techniques to this day. Coaching was not Kennedy's taste, however, and he quit after a season, determined to leave the game behind him.

He would face one final temptation. The Leafs were no better in 1957–58 than in the previous year and during a game at the Gardens, Harold Ballard, one of the club's directors, asked Kennedy to replace Billy Reay as coach of the Leafs. Conn Smythe even made a trip to Kennedy's horse farm in Nobleton, but Kennedy would not be moved. Reay coached the Leafs until he was replaced by Punch Imlach.

"I'd had enough," Kennedy said. "It's a pressure job and I wasn't going to get rich doing it. I never regretted it. I had had enough of living in a fishbowl."

Leaving hockey allowed Kennedy to accommodate a lifelong love of horses. He first accepted a steward's job with the Ontario Racing Commission and then became the chief of security for the Ontario Jockey Club. He owned his own stable in St. Mary's for a time before taking on the job at Fort Erie. At 69, retirement looms only in the distant future. "The Jockey Club at this point in time and for the past few years has left it entirely up to me. That's subject to change. If they feel my efficiency is dropping, they could ask me to retire and that's fine. If and when I do retire, I feel I'd like to get a brood-mare and other horses."

If asked to write his hockey obituary, Kennedy would write only one word—player. From his days at the White Arena, it is all he has wanted to be. No more, no less.

It was not particularly lucrative. His first contract paid him $3,500 a season. His last was worth $25,000.

But he says, "For me, it was a dream come true to play in the National Hockey League. Being a captain, being inducted into the Hall of Fame, as honorable as those might be, it was incidental really. It wasn't something I set out to do. All I wanted was the opportunity to prove myself against my peers."

The emotion is back again, and Teeder Kennedy's eyes glisten for a moment. "If I had continued in university or got a degree or got training in the business world and then played professional hockey, I might have been better off," he says. "But I have absolutely no regrets. It's a dream come true."

For an instant, his voice wavers. Then his expression is strong, sure and ageless, and the smile returns. "But what a dream come true."

CHAPTER 4

GEORGE ARMSTRONG

CAPTAIN, 1957–1969

T he voice on the other end of the telephone line is cordial, gentle and resolute.

"I suggest," said George Armstrong, "that you make my chapter very short."

"George, the problem is that your career was too good to ignore."

"The problem," corrects George Armstrong, "is that you are writing a book on it."

In June, 1961, Gary Lautens, then a sportswriter for the *Hamilton Spectator*, wrote of George Armstrong, "He hopes for security but would play hockey for nothing because of his love for a sport with only one drawback—a spotlight which embarrasses him."

And embarrasses him still.

"Ah, the older we get the better we think we were," Armstrong said. "Honestly, I don't do card shows, I don't do promotions. If I don't do it for other people, I can't turn around and do it for you."

George Armstrong is a congenial man with a history of overachieving. He was and is enormously well liked, and he has something to say to everyone during his strolls through Maple Leaf Gardens. "He was liked by everyone, all the players," said former teammate Allan Stanley. "He was liked by management, he was liked by owners, he was liked by the press. He was a buffer between everybody."

Humor, always humor, is the first characteristic teammates mention when describing Armstrong.

"He'd walk around the dressing room with no teeth in. He looked like Popeye except he had string-bean arms and string bean legs and a pot," recalled one-time teammate Jim McKenny. "He couldn't go by the full-length mirror without giving a flex. He always called himself Digger. He'd say 'Digger, you're beautiful.'"

The memory of it still convulses McKenny. "He'd be looking at himself like he was Marilyn Monroe."

In airports, Armstrong would plant himself near a player and mimic his mannerisms for his teammates' amusement. When Punch Imlach delivered blistering dressing room pep talks, Armstrong would make faces behind his back. Inevitably, whichever persona Armstrong was assuming that day—Digger and Chiefy-Cat were his two favorites—was the butt of the joke.

Armstrong captained four Stanley Cup champions, the most in Maple Leaf history, and lacked none of the fire of the captains who came before him. He was a leader. He did not harangue or challenge the other players; he did not impose his will on anyone. McKenny, in the middle of an alcohol-ravaged career, was never lectured by Armstrong although the two roomed together for a year.

"He accepted me for the person I was," McKenny said. "He didn't tell anyone to do anything."

Armstrong inspired loyalty not through intimidation nor zeal but through admiration. Always dogged and often ferocious on the ice, he overcame a plodding skating style to become one of the franchise's most valuable contributors.

"That," said longtime Montreal forward Claude Larose, a player who went into the corners countless times with Armstrong, "was one tough SOB."

After the game, he went back to being the laugh-a-minute man.

Comedy is an indispensable part of team chemistry. It helps reinforce discipline, breaks up the tedium and builds a sense of exclusivity, of community. It is communication without lectures. While familiar routines provide comfort to the listeners, they offer little insight into the speaker. A joker operates at both the center of a group and at arm's length from the others. Comedy is an outsider's tool. Perhaps it is natural that comedy is what George Armstrong is best remembered for.

Because he is of mixed heritage, Irish and Native Canadian, Armstrong grew up an outsider and has said he encountered racism growing up. While this is hardly a surprise, he has nonetheless rarely discussed it publicly. His mother, Alice Armstrong, once told an interviewer that George's confusion over his heritage was the foundation of his remarkable work ethic.

"He was with my mother, who was a full Indian, and while George was not aware of what he was—white, Indian or what—he was ashamed to be seen with his grandmother because she was different. That's why he has been working so hard, he told me. He said to me that no matter what he was, he won't ever be ashamed."

Armstrong is known universally as Chief, a nickname that might inspire pride in some Native Canadians and offend others. When Armstrong suffered an injury in 1952, the *Globe and Mail*'s Al Nickleson wrote, "Heap bad medicine ball knocked Big Chief George Armstrong out of the Maple Leaf lineup today and bared a glaring problem along the left boards."

The nickname was perfect. It expressed his uniqueness and set him apart while bringing him into the group.

As a Toronto Maple Leaf, Armstrong has found universal acceptance. Had he gone directly into private life after ending his playing days, his work ethic and drive would be the only memory held by the public. This perception would be incomplete; Armstrong allowed greater glimpses into his personality after he stopped playing.

Armstrong never wanted to coach the Leafs and, when he finally had to take the job, he did everything he could to get himself fired. When Harold Ballard obliged him in August, 1989, Armstrong was tickled. One of the Leafs' legendary leaders, he didn't and doesn't want to lead any more.

"I want to be plain George Armstrong again, where I can say stupid, dumb things and nobody will quote me in the media," Armstrong said after his dismissal. "That would be just terrific."

There is an irony in all of this—the dressing room jester was never happy-go-lucky. George Armstrong has had ulcers from the age of 19. He is, in fact, an extroverted loner and that contradiction is puzzling, even to some of his oldest friends.

"I don't know how to explain it," said Johnny Bower, Armstrong's roommate for a decade. "That's just the way he is. He likes people and everything else, but he's a very reserved person."

Armstrong's insistence on privacy isn't the result of an overblown ego. In fact, it's just the opposite. He became a Hall of Fame player by never believing he could be one. Now that he is, he continues to disbelieve.

"He's been to the Hockey Hall of Fame once, maybe twice," said longtime teammate Billy Harris. "He said to me, 'I feel out of place when guys like Beliveau are there and Howe.' He was being sincere. He said 'I'm just not in the same class as those superstars.' He's a very humble man in a peculiar way and I think that has a lot to do with him wanting to be private. He's a bit of a recluse."

The hockey-card shows that Armstrong refuses to attend could generate thousands of dollars a night for hellos and handshakes. They would be easy money for someone whose frugality was always a long-running in-house comedy routine. But the answer is always no.

The press conference naming Doug Gilmour as the new Leafs' captain was one of the few events Armstrong has agreed to attend. He is true to his word. He is determined to be plain George Armstrong.

George Armstrong was born July 6, 1930, in Bowland's Bay, a ten-house northern Ontario community in the shadow of Sudbury, but he spent most of his childhood in the town of Falconbridge. His mother, Alice, is an Algonquin who never received a formal education but taught herself to read and write. His father, Fred, was an Irishman who worked in the nickel mine, mostly underground, for 40 years. The two met at a company dance and never really left Falconbridge. Fred, who died in 1988, called square dances and Alice hired out a few days a week as a domestic.

George Armstrong distinguished himself early on the rinks. A local man, Bob Wilson, wrote the Leafs and recommended that they scout Tod Sloan who lived three doors away from Armstrong. After Sloan scored five goals in a Toronto tournament and signed with the organization, Wilson was hired as a part-time scout. His next tip was Armstrong, then playing for the Copper Cliff Redmen. Wilson was also the scout who recommended that the Leafs sign Tim Horton.

The Leafs added Armstrong's name to their protected list and promptly forgot about him. When Stratford's Junior A team, the Kroehlers, needed an extra hand they contacted Toronto. Although Conn Smythe had never seen Armstrong play, he noticed him on his prospect list and sent him to Stratford. The 17-year-old Armstrong got room, board, $3 a week, a new suit and a $500 bonus. The Kroehlers got the league's scoring champion and most valuable player. Armstrong spent the next season with the junior Toronto Marlboros and moved up to the senior Marlies during the drive to the Allan Cup. He scored 19 goals and added 19 assists in the club's march to the 1949 title. In all, Armstrong recorded 250 points in 120 junior games with the Kroehlers and Marlies. He seemed a can't-miss professional prospect.

During the 1950 Allan Cup, the Marlboros were on a sight-seeing tour and stopped at Alberta's Stoney Indian Reserve. The band, according to the media of the day, nicknamed Armstrong "Big Chief Shoot the Puck" and presented him with a headdress. He has been the Chief ever since.

Armstrong signed a professional contract in 1950 with the Leafs for a minimum of $7,000. Because players then did not use professional agents, Armstrong, desperate for advice, brought along his mother.

Armstrong scored only 15 goals in his rookie American League season but, the next year, 1951–52, he scored 30 goals and picked up 29 assists in 50 AHL games, earning a promotion to the Leafs for the final 20 games of the regular season. In his first NHL game, Armstrong converted a pass from Max Bentley to score his first goal in a 3–2 victory over the Canadiens. That same night, he learned the dangers of candor with the media.

"They asked me how I compared the NHL and the AHL," Armstrong told Lautens of the *Hamilton Spectator*. "I told them that I didn't see much difference except that the NHL players were probably a little wiser. I went 15 games without scoring a goal after that. One day I passed Mr. Smythe and he said, "If this league's no tougher than the AHL, let's see you score some more goals.' I didn't score again until the last game when I got two."

Armstrong inherited number 10, made famous by Syl Apps. Like the number 27 that Darryl Sittler inherited from Frank Mahovlich, "10" came with a special legacy and corresponding pressures. Giving Armstrong that number underscored the regard in which Smythe held him. Later, Smythe would pay Armstrong the ultimate compliment. He named one of his horses Big Chief Army after him. The only other players Smythe chose for this honor were Charlie Conacher (Big Blue Bomber) and Jean Beliveau (Le Gros Bill).

Early on in his career, Armstrong was eager to parlay his salary into long-term security. He planned to buy two house lots in Sudbury, build on them and then sell them. Instead Smythe convinced him to invest $6,000 in shares in the Gardens. He bought 250 shares which he later sold for $100,000. To celebrate, Armstrong bought his dad a Studebaker.

As a rookie, Armstrong's place in the team's hierarchy was set. He roomed with Bentley, one of the era's stars, and also served as his caddy and valet. When Bentley didn't feel like practicing, Armstrong would inform coach Joe Primeau. "I was thankful for the privilege," Armstrong said later. "It was like running errands for the prime minister."

In his first full year, he scored 14 times and collected 25 points but, after seasons of 17 and 10 goals, it was clear he would never repeat the numbers he had compiled before reaching Toronto. Some held him up as an example of a junior phenom who would never pan out as an NHLer. Armstrong's size (he entered the league at 6'1" and 195 pounds) and instincts had allowed him to dominate the junior and minor pro game, but they were no longer enough of an advantage at the NHL level. In fact, when he reached the NHL, Armstrong discovered his package of skills was thoroughly unremarkable. While he possessed excellent balance and could skate acceptably in a straight line, he had little speed and less maneuverability. The only time he seemed to possess even serviceable quickness was when he had the puck.

"We had a standing joke," said Allan Stanley. "He was no Sonja Henie. When he was going down the ice against a defenseman, it always looked like he was going to fall down. But he always ended up on the other side of the defenseman with a good shot on net or a good chance to make a play."

The feebleness of his shot was another source of fun. "He had pretty good hands but he couldn't break a paper bag with his shot," Bower said.

"The Chief is the only guy in the National Hockey League who can shoot the puck in the net and the net won't budge," laughed practice goalie Gerry McNamara.

It was all true. Armstrong was a middling stickhandler with nowhere near the control enjoyed by gifted attackers such as Dave Keon or Frank Mahovlich. Somehow, though, the total of George Armstrong, the player, outweighed the sum of his parts. Despite his limitations, he would occasionally score showstopping goals, and he developed into a player who was always dependable and occasionally dangerous. Often set up as if he were the third defenseman, he was routinely the deepest forward in his own zone. Armstrong was a quick and steady passer who protected the puck well and moved it efficiently out of his own end.

"I've read where people said he didn't have a lot of talent and I've never agreed with that," said Hall of Fame goaltender Glenn Hall. "He was an excellent player who was very dangerous in front of the net."

"I remember he beat everyone on the Montreal Canadiens on the way from the blue line," recalled writer Scott Young.

"He would show them the puck, pull it back, put it between his feet, pull the goalie and score. I was talking to Tim Horton later, and Horton said, 'I was back at the blue line watching and I had to laugh. He's done it so often.'"

Like Kennedy, Armstrong was nourished by the Maple Leafs' tradition of defensive vigilance created by Conn Smythe and Hap Day.

"He played the Leafs' old system—up and down the wing, up and down the wing," said Stanley. "People talk about a system now but a team with a system was the Toronto Maple Leafs. They used to call them the clutch and grabs. No skating room across the ice. The Chief was a product of that. He looked after his wing; somebody else could look after the other wing."

"I think he was one of these guys who would never commit himself out of position," said Hall of Famer Pierre Pilote. "He played the game very smartly and he almost never got trapped. If he got caught out of position, boy, he put his head down and came back hard."

Armstrong's commitment to the game was unsurpassed. He took extensive notes and, before every game, would write down all on-ice possibilities and how he would deal with them. He became an expert on angles, forcing opponents out of position and neutralizing players on his side of the rink.

"His game was built on percentages," Pilote said. "It was up-and-down hockey and taking a chance only when he knew he had a better chance of winning the opening."

If Armstrong could not rule the slot, he would own the corners. Competitors call him one of the best cornermen ever, big enough to tie up opponents and protect the puck, determined to make the play.

"He was strong in the corner," Bower said. "When he crossed his stick over the other guy's stick, George was so strong there was no way the other guy could move."

"He just had a gift along the boards and in the corners," said former linemate Ron Ellis. "And he was able to make the play in front of the net once he got the puck."

Armstrong rarely slept the night before a game, preferring to read, plan and smoke. He was often just dozing off at 6 a.m. when the rest of the Leafs were getting up to catch a train. Bower would often wake up to find an extra blanket wrapped around him.

Although he was now a regular, the 1950s were largely undistinguished for the Leafs and Armstrong. After their 1950–51 Cup triumph, the Leafs did not return to the final until 1958–59.

Armstrong was 27 when he became captain in 1957–58, succeeding Kennedy. Over the previous two years, three players had worn the C: Kennedy in his short-lived comeback, Sid Smith and Jim Thomson, who had been traded because of union activities. Armstrong had seen firsthand the perils of the position. But Armstrong had both the standing among his teammates and the ideal temperament for the job.

"A lot of guys, you make them captain and all of a sudden they feel a responsibility to have team meetings and do this and do that," said Billy Harris. "I played three years with Armstrong when he wasn't a captain. They made him captain and it didn't change him."

Still, neither Armstrong nor the Maple Leafs had done anything to signal their intention to become serious Stanley Cup challengers. But Punch Imlach moved from assistant general manager to general manager and finally to coach/GM in 1958–59, and the Leafs, who hadn't made the playoffs the previous fall, advanced to the finals before falling to a strong Montreal team. The following year, they again made the finals and again lost to the Habs.

Armstrong and Imlach would combine for Stanley Cups in 1962, 1963, 1964 and 1967. Armstrong would produce 26 goals and 60 points in 110 playoff games, including the empty net insurance goal that sealed the 1967 Cup victory over Montreal. He would reach the 20-goal plateau four times in his career, all after Imlach's arrival. With a dependable scoring touch added to his steady cornerwork and genial manner, Armstrong flowered into the consummate leader.

It was an unlikely partnership between the flinty coach and the jester captain, but it was integral to the Leafs' success.

"Chief was a tremendous power of example," Jim McKenny said. "He worked harder than anybody else in practice. When they told us to go around twice, he'd go around three times. When they told us to break the blue line, Chief would always break and go 20 yards further."

In 1961, Conn Smythe called Armstrong "the best captain, as a captain, the Leafs have ever had."

"I think Armstrong led by example more than any of the other people who came along later," said Scott Young. "If you watch the way Keon played, you had to play up to him. Armstrong wasn't as obviously skilled as Keon but Armstrong had the combination of some super hockey skills plus an attitude that made him a great captain."

Imlach, especially in his later years with the Maple Leafs, ruled with an iron fist. However, he sought not to divide but to unite the team, not to fragment opinion but to unify it. He was the ultimate bad cop but he needed a foil, a good cop, and no one was better than his captain.

"You know, Punch was a very strict guy," Bower said. "Chief handled it really well. He'd say we've got to win or play well, otherwise you know where we'll end up. And Punch would put anybody on the bench or trade them."

Bower often saw Armstrong huddling with Clancy and Imlach. "I'm sure George talked them out of a lot of trades. I don't think I ever heard him want to let a player go. He was the captain. He wanted to keep everybody."

When a player went AWOL, it was Armstrong who gave advice and acted as intermediary.

"Jim Dorey jumped ship one day when we were going by train from Montreal to Chicago," recalled McKenny. "We hit Windsor and we realized Flipper wasn't on the train. He wasn't feeling well. When we got to Chicago, the first thing Chief did was call him at home. He told him to apologize and suck up and nothing would come of it."

"Armstrong wasn't a spy. We trusted George and he was on our side," said Harris. "If Imlach jumped on somebody, he was there to defend the guy."

Armstrong used psychology with slumping players. When a teammate expressed worries about his play, Armstrong usually gave a list of everything he himself had done wrong. Why should he feel insecure, the player would reason, if the captain had the same concerns and, more important, knew he would soon play through them?

"He not only led on the ice but off the ice," said winger Bob Pulford, now the general manager of the Chicago Blackhawks. "He involved players. He cared about them and made sure everyone did their best just as he did on the ice. If you're going to paint the criteria of the ideal captain, he was it."

Armstrong's game aged beautifully. There wasn't much speed to lose and, despite a lifetime of smoking, he remained strong and durable, especially in the corners and when killing penalties. Armstrong churning up the ice to score the insurance goal in the last game of the 1967 final against Montreal is the defining moment of the Leafs' four-Cup 1960s run, the last hurrah of the six-team era. By then, Imlach had lost virtually all his influence with the team. Armstrong and a cadre of veterans, Pulford, Bob Baun and Allan Stanley, ran the dressing room and left the bench to Imlach.

Armstrong first announced his retirement in 1967 when the Leafs left him unprotected in the expansion draft. The move was actually a ploy to keep him off the roster of an expansion team, allowing the Leafs to protect a younger player. Armstrong went undrafted and returned to score 13 goals and add 21 assists in the first expansion season. Armstrong quit after training camp the following year and the Leafs played without a permanent captain. The job was kept open for Armstrong and his jersey was left hanging in his empty locker. On December 2, 1968, after watching the Leafs lose 3–1 to New York, he called Imlach and told him he would come back.

He quit again after that year, again to be lured back after training camp in 1969. More than a few people in the media believed that Armstrong's ambivalence lay in a desire for a raise.

"Each time, Armstrong said he retired because he didn't think he could help the team," wrote the *Toronto Star*'s Red Burnett. "But the real reason was money."

Armstrong scored just seven goals in 59 games in 1970–71. Finally, at 40, he retired for good.

His 12 seasons as captain, from 1957–58 to 1968–69, still stand as the longest tenure in NHL history. Detroit's Alex Delvecchio (11 seasons), the New York Rangers' Bill Cook (11), Wayne Gretzky with both the Edmonton Oilers and the L.A. Kings (11), Jean Beliveau (10), and Rod Langway (10) of the Washington Capitals are the only other players to have double-digit seasons as captains. The man who never led the Leafs in goals and led only once in points retired as the club's leader in career goals, points and games played. While other players scored in geysers, Armstrong's goals came in drips.

George Armstrong had two career hat tricks. Darryl Sittler, the Leafs' reigning goals and points leader, had 16.

Of all the Maple Leafs' captains, Armstrong's career is the most difficult to quantify. And, while none of his statistical feats were outstanding, he was inducted into the Hall of Fame in 1975. Armstrong's most impressive number, 1,187 games played, stood only 25th on the all-time list going into the 1994–95 season. His 296 goals was the 99th best in NHL history. He sat 116th in assists and 99th in points. Ninety-nine different players have appeared in more playoff games, and his playoff total of 26 goals ranked 121st. Even when compared to other right-wingers, Armstrong's regular season statistics are unspectacular. He is 35th in career goals, 24th in assists and 26th in points. His playoff scoring totals are similarly humble.

But, of course, no statistics are kept for battles won in the corners, opposing forwards shut down or rookies counseled on trains.

Armstrong's gift was the ability to endure and to win. Before 1994–1995, only four right-wingers—Gordie Howe (1,767 games), Ron Stewart (1,353), Ed Westfall (1,227) and Eric Nesterenko (1,219)—had played more games. Of that group, Armstrong and Howe won four Stanley Cups. Stewart played on three Stanley Cup winners, Westfall on two and Eric Nesterenko on one. The Leafs' Mike Gartner, who passed Armstrong in games played in 1994–95, has not won a Cup.

Armstrong seemed an excellent candidate to stay in the game as a coach. After his retirement, Armstrong coached the Toronto Marlboros to Memorial Cups in 1972–73 and 1974–75 but it was not, in fact, a job that suited him. While it wasn't really necessary to scare or intimidate juniors, his favorite practice drill was hog, Armstrong never developed the ability to cut a player, in junior or in the pros, without bleeding himself.

"It hurts me when a kid comes up to me and asks what he's doing wrong," he said in 1977. "How do I tell him he just hasn't got it and will never become a hockey player?"

Armstrong wanted to scout for the Leafs but a position never materialized. He hung on as coach and general manager of the Marlies until 1978 and then gave the coaching reins to Bill White.

"I've been saying I wanted out since they gave me the job so I decided it was about time I put up or shut up," Armstrong told the *Globe and Mail* in September, 1978. A short while later he said he left the job because the amount of fighting sickened him.

"I don't have any proof but I'm certain that some coaches just send their players out to fight. That bothers me so much. It really makes me sick to my stomach."

Armstrong stayed for a few more weeks and then quit as the general manager. He had assumed that, after more than three decades in the Toronto organization, he would be able to resign one position and maintain the other. He discovered he was wrong when he went to pick up his cheque at the Gardens and found that his name had been taken off the payroll list.

"Sure, I quit because I wasn't getting paid," Armstrong told reporters. "But the real reason I quit hockey was that I couldn't stand the way the other coaches act. My original intention was to stay on as general manager and help Bill for a few months, but I just felt that if I wasn't getting paid, I better leave and try to find some work."

Former Leafs' general manager Gord Stellick said Armstrong turned Harold Ballard down when Ballard ordered him to coach the Maple Leafs instead of the Marlies in 1977. Armstrong appeared at the NHL draft but soon after managed to escape. Ballard hired Roger Neilson instead.

"Chief went back to coaching the Marlies but Harold made

it miserable for him," Stellick said. "What impressed me was that he had stood up, he had taken enough from Harold. I always remembered that and, when you added that to what you knew about him as the captain of the Leafs, I saw him as a principled guy."

In 1978, after 32 years in the Leafs' organization, Armstrong took a scouting job with the Quebec Nordiques. He worked for the Nordiques for ten years until the club, wanting younger men in their organization, let him go.

One of the trademarks of the Harold Ballard era was the ruthless disposal of all traces of the Maple Leafs' proud past. Everything from Foster Hewitt's gondola to the dressing room plaques was trashed, but the most disposable commodities of all were the players. Many, such as Armstrong and later Dave Keon, were dismissed as if they were disobedient paper boys.

When he took over the general manager's job in 1988, Stellick made reconciling with the past a priority. Plans to bring Darryl Sittler back into the front office fizzled, but Stellick had more luck with Armstrong who returned as a scout. He was, however, quickly swept up from a spot in the chorus to a starring role. When Ballard fired coach John Brophy without thinking of a successor, a favorite habit of his, he turned to Armstrong.

Armstrong gave in. "Chief once told me, 'How can I say no to a dying man?'" one friend said.

Armstrong didn't want the job and his half a season was a sham. He actually coached the team for only a handful of games before giving all real authority to assistant coach Garry Lariviere.

"The first three or four games he actually coached, he even dug up old hotel notepads he had written on when he was a player," said Stellick. "Then we had this loss one or two games before Christmas and we were dead last and out of the playoff picture. He just found it too much and gave it to Garry Lariviere. That wasn't the idea, to make him [Lariviere] the de facto head coach."

Behind the bench, wrote the *Toronto Sun*'s Jim O'Leary, Armstrong was "looking like a tourist lost in a Manhattan rush hour."

The Leafs went 17–26–4 under Armstrong but Stellick had to insist that Armstrong not be rehired. Armstrong had clearly surrendered the coaching job but was unwilling to risk Ballard's wrath by quitting. Although Armstrong had made himself the worst coach in the National Hockey League, it was left to Stellick to take the heat.

"The more I told Harold that we're looking at the coaching situation, the more angry he got at me," Stellick said. "Then finally, when I did squawk, it all fell back on me."

Stellick surrendered what little credit he had left with Ballard to convince him not to rehire Armstrong. "I misjudged that Chief would let it [the situation] go on so long," said Stellick, "but it's kind of unfair to say. The man was 60 years old, he had lost his job a couple of months before. It was a whole different kettle of fish from the proud captain of the Toronto Maple Leafs."

Stellick signed Armstrong to a new three-year contract so that, even if he didn't coach, Armstrong would still be paid.

If Armstrong himself couldn't confront Ballard, he would use the media to get what he wanted. He all but publicly challenged Ballard to dismiss him by telling reporters that if the Leafs fired him, "nobody else in the world" would bother hiring him. When Ballard finally agreed to make a coaching change in August, 1988, Armstrong was relieved. Ballard was obligated to pay him for three years; Armstrong's tenure with the organization in a less visible capacity was now secure.

"It [the firing] is not something that displeases me a great deal," Armstrong said. "I had tried to be loyal to the organization and do whatever they asked of me. I loved Maple Leaf Gardens but I disliked being expected to explain things to the news media. How can you explain to reporters the reasons for our team's losses when, really, you don't know the answers yourself?"

Ballard now had Stellick squarely in his sights. He made Armstrong director of player personnel, thus promoting him over Stellick. Armstrong also agreed to Ballard's order that Armstrong, not Stellick, announce the Leafs' choices at that summer's amateur draft. It was a humiliating position for Stellick who quit the Leafs soon after. Armstrong's survival skills may have been undiminished by time but they didn't win him universal admiration.

"It's as if when Armstrong stripped away his Leafs uniform years ago he also stripped away his pride," wrote Jim O'Leary.

Ballard died in April, 1990, leaving Armstrong free to return to a scouting job, a position he still holds.

And so the quiet he has long coveted has finally descended on George Armstrong. With Cliff Fletcher running the Maple Leafs, sanity has returned to the Gardens and Armstrong can go back to watching hockey players and writing down how they do.

Last March, *Toronto Star* hockey writer Damien Cox looked up from his seat in the press box to see Armstrong steaming by.

"Hi, Chief," said Cox.

"Screw you," snarled George Armstrong in mock anger as he passed.

Cox, familiar with Armstrong's humor, burst into laughter. "That Chief," he said. "He's a great guy."

CHAPTER 5

DAVE KEON

CAPTAIN 1969–75

Dave Keon came into the world in 1940, the same year as penicillin and the blitzkrieg. He became a Toronto Maple Leaf in 1960, the year of John Kennedy and widely available birth control pills. When he was dismissed from the Leafs in 1975, Jimmy Hoffa was about to disappear and Patricia Hearst was still missing.

Understanding Dave Keon means understanding the times in which he played because the wild changes of that era extended to hockey. Keon's career spanned the dying days of the original six and the comparative salary boom of the World Hockey Association. His has been a life and a career of transition and, often, of inflexibility to change.

Dave Michael Keon's father, David Herbert, spent almost all of his working life as a miner. Keon's mother, Laura, was a teacher. Their oldest son was an athlete armed with unimpeachable intelligence and a backbone as rigid as any ore pulled from the ground.

As a player, Keon was a skilled craftsman in an era of declining workmanship. He had the luck of playing for the

Maple Leafs during their finest years and the misfortune of being cast as the lead carpenter for a crumbling kingdom.

Keon was the among the least penalized superstars in NHL history but he was among the league's fiercest competitors and most acerbic personalities.

While he stood only 5'9" and weighed 165 pounds, he went into the corners recklessly, finished his checks religiously and led the Leafs in hits almost every night. The quintessential team player on the ice, he was disliked by many teammates.

Keon remained the same—stern, aloof and dedicated—throughout his captaincy and beyond. The player whose name, for a generation of fans, is synonymous with the Leafs, attended his first Leafs' function in 15 years in 1990. He lives in Palm Beach Gardens, Florida, and dabbles in commercial real estate in West Palm Beach. Keon almost never gives interviews and has little contact with hockey.

"He's not a friendly guy unless he knows you," said longtime friend and *Hockey Night in Canada* color commentator Harry Neale. "He has the attitude, you're my enemy until you prove otherwise, rather than you're a good guy until you prove otherwise. He's got a surly side to him and it isn't becoming at times but, as a friend, I'd defend him to the nth degree."

Keon is believed to still be angry at the Maple Leafs for their cavalier dismissal of him, but he has never spoken publicly of his feelings about the team's management, past or present, nor of the place he holds in the pantheon of Maple Leafs' greats.

To many, Keon represents the generation of original six players who are angry at a league that exploited them and stole their pension money. "Hull, Keon, Gordie Howe—these guys gave a pile to this game," said 13-year original six veteran Bert Olmstead, "but not to have some son of a bitch steal their money."

Keon is believed to be one of many players who resented the

next generation of players, the ones who benefited from the WHA-inspired salary wars of the 1970s. Lanny McDonald, who roomed with Keon as a rookie, wrote in *Lanny* that Keon, then the Maple Leafs' captain, treated him coldly and did nothing to ease his rocky transition into the NHL.

"I'll be glad to talk to you about Darryl," McDonald said, "but if you want anything on Dave Keon, you'll have to ask someone else."

"He was short," said teammate Jim McKenny, "both in height and in temperament. With him, it was all out all the time. Chief [George Armstrong] didn't expect it from everybody else but David did. One time during an exhibition game, the two of us stood there screaming at each other, him on the bench and me on the ice. I yelled, 'Go screw yourself.' The next day, I was in Rochester."

McKenny, along with many others, came to see Keon's harshness as positive. "When I first went to the Leafs, he treated me terrible. I hated his guts," McKenny said. "By the end I was a pretty good friend of his."

Harold Ballard believed Keon was a poor captain and in this he was not alone. Many couldn't see past the relentlessly gruff exterior, the fanatical pursuit of excellence and the stubborn resistance to compromise that made him play with the same shin pads for 20 years and refuse to change his brushcut until years after it had gone hopelessly out of style.

"Yeah, he was tough," said teammate Rick Ley, now the coach of the Vancouver Canucks. "But he didn't do it to be cruel. He did it because, if you're not giving what you have to give, you're letting the other people in the dressing room down. He was a competitor, he wanted to win and he wanted to be successful. I would be much more respectful of a person who led by example than one who just did a lot of talking."

Dave Keon grew up in Noranda, Quebec, not far from the Ontario-Quebec border. Dave's dad, David Sr., lived with his grandparents after his mother died in his early teens. He stayed with them in the Sudbury area where the mining industry offered prospects for hard-working men. He worked for years in and around the mining industry, setting up work sites and camps. Dave Sr. was 49 when he married a 32-year-old schoolteacher, Laura Sloan. She was a brilliant woman, the eldest of ten children (nine of them girls) and a member of the first graduating class of the Ottawa Normal School.

While both were descendants of Irish Catholic settlers in the Ottawa valley, David and Laura were very different from each other. Dave Sr. was illiterate and stubbornly refused to learn to read, even when his wife was tutoring other adults in the family home. Instead he insisted his six children read the newspapers aloud to him, a practice the Keon siblings, unaware their father could not read, considered an exercise to improve their reading. Despite Dave Sr.'s unwillingness to learn to read, he and Laura shared a respect for education. Dave, the hockey player, is the only one of their children without a post-graduate university degree.

The Keon children grew up in a modest duplex in Noranda. Their home had three bedrooms; one for Laura and David, one for the four girls and one for the two boys, who shared a bed.

The family had two religions. One was Catholicism, and the rosary was said every night after dinner. "Work was the other religion in our family," said Jim Keon, Dave's brother and a Leafs' prospect during the 1960s.

David Sr. was a diligent employee who worked at the Quemont Mines in Noranda until he was 73. He died in 1973 at the age of 83. Laura died in 1994 at 87.

"David is much like my dad," Jim Keon said. "He's

extremely disciplined. Imagine in 35 below weather at 5 a.m. getting up and stoking the furnace and walking to work, which was two miles away. My dad was one of the true professionals, the people who realized they had a job to do, that people were depending on it. They got up and did it. You can see it in all of us but certainly in David. Those disciplines were there from early on."

The eldest son was raised strictly and carefully. "I know that, as young fledgling parents, your first child is going to be perfect," said Jim Keon, a Montrealer and himself the father of two girls. "Later, you tend to back off and realize there's a lot of luck involved. David was brought up pretty strictly. He had to endure a lot of expectations put on him. The theory was, if you brought the first one up right, the rest would follow."

At two outdoor rinks a block away from the family home Keon developed his remarkable talents. Until his mid-teens, he played only one game a week indoors. At 12, he told his parents he was going to become a professional hockey player. When Keon refused to consider any other occupation, his parents reluctantly agreed that if he finished his schooling, he could pursue hockey as a career.

Keon's skating and skill were quickly noticed. At 15 he was a standout at a Detroit Red Wings' tryout camp and was invited to play for the Wings' Junior B team in Burlington, Ontario. But Laura Keon wasn't ready to let her son pursue hockey without completing his education. She also thought he was too young to leave home.

"My mother told me that if I went, I'd have to pack my own bag," Keon once told an interviewer. "I got her meaning so I stayed home another winter."

Vince Thompson, a Leafs' bird dog, was coaching the Noranda Juveniles. He wired Bob Davidson, the Leafs' chief scout: "Grab this kid or he'll be haunting you ten years from now." Thompson didn't know it but in fact he was selling Keon way short. Davidson spent $1,000 to make the Leafs the sponsors of Thompson's team. Under the rules of the time, the Leafs now had first crack at all the players.

When Keon showed himself to be an excellent prospect, Toronto's St. Michael's College School proved to be an acceptable compromise between the ambitions of Dave and his parents. Keon could continue his schooling at St. Mike's, fulfilling his parents' desire for him to receive a Catholic education, and at the same time learn hockey from one of the game's foremost teachers, Father David Bauer. Players on the school team were automatically affiliated with the Maple Leafs. "The Toronto Maple Leafs had the two best recruiting tools in the business," *Toronto Star* hockey writer Frank Orr has said. "Foster Hewitt and the Basilian fathers."

Keon had obvious offensive gifts—his skating and stick-handling seemed heaven-sent—but offense alone, no matter how prodigious, did not automatically qualify a prospect for a seat on the Leafs' bench. Keon's game needed polish. The late Bob Goldham, who coached Keon for three seasons at the school, felt Keon was poor defensively until his fourth and final year at St. Mike's. "Father David Bauer, who was the manager of the team, and I used to tell him he'd never make the NHL unless he learned to check," Goldham told *Star* writer Jim Proudfoot in 1971. "Privately, I felt much different. I knew he couldn't miss because he skated so beautifully and could score so easily. And I knew he could check just as easily if he'd put his mind to it. But that seemed to be the trouble. He didn't seem very interested in checking, maybe because scoring came so naturally to him."

Keon eventually learned defense and became the embodiment of everything Father Bauer, a Hockey Hall of Famer, had tried to impart. He studied positioning relentlessly, always had his body squared to the oncoming player and learned to stop instead of turn away when his check stopped skating.

"Defensively, there was no comparison between the Keon who left St. Mike's in the spring of 1960 and the Keon who reported to the Leafs that fall," Goldham said.

"The way I remember it, I got the message a year earlier when the Leafs didn't bring me up," Keon has said. "I thought they were going to. I improved my checking that last season at St. Mike's but Goldie's right. I shaped up a lot over that summer simply because I realized what had to be done and I made up my mind to do it." After his final season at St. Mike's, Keon played four professional games with the Leafs' Sudbury affiliate in the Eastern Professional Hockey League, scoring twice and adding two assists. In 1960, at the age of 20, he broke into the NHL as one of the game's best two-way players.

But Keon came close to missing his chance to stick. Punch Imlach, then the club's coach and general manager, was planning to send Keon to Rochester in the American Hockey League on the principle that, no matter how talented the player, he had to serve some apprenticeship. Bert Olmstead, one of the game's all-time great cornermen, interceded. It wasn't charity; Olmstead was unrelenting in his desire to win and he had little use for those who didn't share his conviction. He saw in Keon a kindred spirit wrapped in a small body that might not survive the weaker refereeing of the AHL.

"Imlach said there's no player who's going to make this team from junior," Olmstead said. "I told him he was crazier than hell. I told him, 'If you keep him, by the end of the year he'll be your best center, and they'll kill him in the American League.' But he didn't keep him because of me. Davey made him change his mind."

Olmstead was right. No one could get the puck off the rookie in scrimmages. Keon collected 20 goals and 45 points in his first year and outdistanced teammate Bob Nevin for the Calder Trophy as rookie of the year. In his second year, he scored 26 goals, finished with 61 points, earned only one minor penalty and was a second-team all-star.

Keon was instrumental in the Leafs' run of three Stanley Cups in the early 1960s. He scored in his first Stanley Cup final game and added an assist as the Leafs handled Chicago four games to two in the 1962 final. In the 1963 final, he scored two shorthanded goals as the Leafs clinched the Cup with a 3–1 win over Detroit.

In 1964, Keon netted all three goals in game seven of the semi-final against Montreal as the Leafs eliminated the Habs and won the game 3–1. Bob Baun scored the overtime winner in game six of the final against Detroit, and the Leafs cruised to a 4–0 win in game seven. Keon, George Armstrong and Gordie Howe tied for the series' lead with four goals, but Keon helped limit Detroit's high-flying centers, Alex Delvecchio and Norm Ullman, to a goal each.

Keon scored 19 times and added ten assists in 36 playoff games as the Leafs won Cups in 1962, 1963 and 1964. Keon would push the Maple Leafs to one more Stanley Cup in 1967, racking up the Conn Smythe Trophy for most valuable player in the playoffs as the Leafs defeated Montreal in six games.

"I don't know any player who did as much damage to the Montreal Canadiens as Dave Keon," noted Red Fisher, the *Montreal Gazette*'s peerless hockey writer who began covering the league in 1957. "Game in and game out, he was the best Leaf I ever saw."

Ironically, Keon's main role model was a Canadien, Henri Richard. "He used to ask me about him. 'Should I pattern myself after Henri?'" recalled Olmstead, who played with both. "He watched and saw what little guys could do. He watched his speed, they were about the same speed, and how he forechecked."

Through the 1960s Keon averaged 23 goals and 54 points per year and broke into the league's top ten scorers only once. The numbers aren't spectacular unless they are qualified. Keon spent most nights neutralizing the competition's number one center.

"I asked him about his career once," said Harry Neale. "He said, 'I can only tell you about Beliveau, Stan Mikita, Delvecchio and whoever the other great centers were. Those are the only guys I ever saw.'"

Keon's game was built on smarts and speed. He was technically a perfect skater. His stride was explosive, his movements precise, quiet and compact. Keon was a master of space. Thanks to his skating, he could close in on a player in a heartbeat. He worked on making himself unpredictable, sometimes darting toward an opponent, sometimes holding back, always changing the tempo.

"Because of his speed, he always gave himself as much room as possible," said Jean Ratelle, a longtime adversary with the New York Rangers. "That's the name of the game. You skate so you can have more room and more time to do things and he did that very, very well. Because of his speed and quickness, let's say on a penalty kill, he could cheat a little bit, he could commit a little deeper but still get back out to the point fast."

Keon was a relentless hockey player. He was the Leafs' premier face-off man, table-setting forechecker and perpetual motion machine.

"One thing—you'd never, ever think this—he'd lead the team every night in hits," said Rick Ley. "He never ran over people but he would set you up. Say he was playing with Bob Pulford and Ron Ellis. If he pushed the player to the left side, they'd never come back on him. His linemates always knew, if

Keon was pushing the opposing player out, you had the guy boxed in."

Ley said that, of all Keon's gifts, his internal compass was the most unfailing. "That's something I've taken into my coaching and he was the best ever at—the game of angles. He knew angles and he'd put you into a spot where he limited your options."

"Trying to move the puck past Keon," Hall of Fame defenseman Bill Gadsby once said, "was about as easy as shaking your shadow in the sunshine."

Once he had the puck, Keon would skate away, free of defensive responsibilities. The marvel of watching Keon was the completeness of his game. "He was smart, fast, an excellent skater," said Gordie Howe. "He had the ability to lay the puck on another guy's stick as neatly as anybody. He could do it all."

His game was so well-rounded that whether he was a better offensive or defensive player was the subject of debate.

"He's a superb checker, everybody knows that," Jacques Plante once told reporters, "but it's his offensive ability that impresses me."

The only weapon missing from Keon's offensive arsenal was an overpowering shot, but he was explosive and resourceful around the net. "I haven't seen any other player move as quickly around the net," Plante said. "The goalie never knows what Davey is going to do next, but he [Keon] knows it all the time. That gives him a big advantage."

Keon studied opponents constantly and was equally obsessive about every detail of his game.

Longtime Leafs' trainer Joe Sgro respected Keon enormously but found him to be the fussiest player he had ever encountered. "We couldn't touch nothing of his equipment unless he asked us to. We couldn't go near it. He was fussy about everything. The stick had to be a certain way, just a slight curve, just enough for you to tell it's a left. He was fussy about his sticks, his gloves, pants, everything. Dave used 14 strands of tape for his handle," recalled Sgro. "He had 'em all counted for the knob of the stick. Just 14, that's it, bango. He was amazing, no one was allowed to tape the sticks. He would take the sticks home and shave them at home, he had a plane and sander at home. He'd take half a dozen home, the next morning they were on the rack."

Keon, Sgro remembered, once became angry because after drying a pair of skates the trainers had inserted the laces differently.

"He was a craftsman, with his equipment, with his stick," recalled teammate Paul Henderson. "He came with a philosophy—you went out there and you gave it your best shot every shift that you had."

Keon was almost impossible to knock out of the lineup. Over his NHL career, Keon played in 1,296 of a possible 1,354 regular season games or about 96 percent. "To me, he was so tough," Jim McKenny said. "I remember, one time he went into the dressing room and there were already two guys hurt. He had dislocated his thumb. He was sitting there, waiting for the trainers to get the thumb pulled out and set. He finally got mad, yanked the thumb out, fixed it himself, grabbed some black tape to keep it in place and went back out. Never said a word on the bench."

Keon played one season without complaint with a knee cartilage torn in training camp, and he would brook no complaints from others.

"If you were whining on the bench, he'd say, 'If you're hurt, get to the room'," McKenny recalled. "He'd never let the other team see he was hurt."

When Bert Olmstead retired in 1962, Keon moved to fill the void left by the hard-nosed veteran.

"Dave told me, when he first went to Toronto he used to get to practice 20 minutes early so he could get out and be on the ice before Bert Olmstead came in," said Harry Neale. "Or he got there two minutes before practice because Olmstead, who he really admired as a player, was a caustic guy who was on his teammates if they didn't have the same attitude he did. And I think Dave kind of became Bert when Bert left."

Jim Keon, who once played an exhibition game on his brother's wing at a Leafs' training camp, agreed. "He yelled at me for 60 minutes," Keon said. "If I was on the boards, he'd yell to stay in the middle. If I went in the middle, he'd yell to stay on the boards. That's the way he was."

When George Armstrong retired in 1969, general manager Jim Gregory, coach John McLellan and King Clancy decided that Keon was the best choice to succeed him as captain. From the beginning, however, the letter was a poor fit. At the press conference to announce Keon's captaincy, the Leafs didn't have a jersey ready. Instead, Sgro pulled an old Armstrong jersey out of mothballs and pinned the sleeves so the number 10 wouldn't be visible to photographers.

Keon assumed the new position in a typically straightforward fashion. "There's something special about being captain, all right, but I'm me and I hope that because I'm captain I won't change," he told reporters. "It is a combination, as I see it, of representing the players and management."

When Harold Ballard took over the Leafs in 1971, Keon had been the captain for two years. The man who represented tradition would soon become the enemy of the man who wanted to tear it down.

Their conflicts often involved money. Keon was a tough negotiator who once signed a new contract just an hour before the face-off of the season opener while Ballard hated paying the going rate for all but a few exceptions. Keon also annoyed

Ballard because he wanted to be paid for personal appearances, a function Leafs' captains had traditionally done for free or for a small honorarium. And Ballard once incensed Keon by commandeering one of his game sticks for a gift.

But when the owner complained about his captain's temperament, he was quickly chastised by the media.

Ballard, wrote Frank Orr, was "obviously figuring the fact that Keon was always in top condition and gave a full effort on every shift didn't set a good example for the Leafs' kids."

Keon's prickly dressing room attitude elicited different responses from different players. Some detested him. Others felt they understood.

"Sometimes it was more in what Dave did than what he said," said Darryl Sittler. "It was his reactions, short little sarcastic things at times, but I think Davey was doing it with the purpose of making a point to the person and trying to get the most out of them. He wasn't doing it to have a negative effect; it was about having a positive effect."

If the definition of a captain begins and ends with on-ice excellence, Keon was the perfect choice.

"He was a great captain," said McKenny. "He played hard every shift. The rougher the game got, the harder he would go."

Although both were from Noranda, Keon met his wife, Lola, while attending St. Mike's. They married in 1960 and eventually had four children, including Dave Keon Jr., by the time Keon was 24. One son, Richard, had breathing problems and lived only eight months, all of them at Sick Children's Hospital.

But by the early 1970s, Keon's marriage was over. He was living away from his family and his private anguish made him even more unapproachable.

"Sometimes, he'd come in and wouldn't say hello or talk to you for a week," Sgro recalled. "He wouldn't talk to anyone.

He had something bothering him. We wouldn't ask him, we'd wait for him to tell us. He was tough that way, really tough. Tough as anybody out there. A whole week and he wouldn't say a word."

"There were nights where you could go in and talk to Keon after a game and he was full of information and ready to come up with it," said Milt Dunnell. "The next night you would come up to him and he wouldn't even reply. He wouldn't even say, 'Well, I don't want to talk'."

Keon's crumbling personal life corresponded with enormous changes in the NHL. Very little had changed for NHL players in the 1940s, '50s and early '60s. The same six franchises were ruled by the same despotic general managers. The game itself had remained practically unaltered since the league adopted the icing rule in 1937.

Although Ted Lindsay, Carl Brewer and others had mobilized NHLers into forming a players' union, steady pressure, trades and owner harassment broke up the association in the late 1950s. Keon's cousin, Tod Sloan, was one of many players traded because of his union activities.

Hockey was played mostly by the sons of miners and farmers who brought a working-class ethic to an unforgiving sport. Rookies were expected to shut up and listen and, if they didn't, they were told to.

"I was sort of like Keon when I broke in [in 1948]," said Olmstead. "You speak when you're spoken to but you don't go in a hole and cover yourself up. You listened."

The powerlessness of the players translated into a sense of resignation that pervaded the league. Jean Beliveau, when playing with a broken jaw, considered wearing a helmet with a face-guard. When Montreal coach Dick Irvin saw it in the dressing room, he smashed it and told the players that anyone who thought about wearing face protection wouldn't see the ice.

Coaching techniques were largely primitive and players were largely self-taught. "Mainly you learned by watching other players and by talking," Olmstead recalled.

Midway into Keon's career, it all changed. The explosion of jobs created by NHL expansion and the arrival of the WHA caused the pendulum to swing toward player agents and the newly minted Players' Association. Rookies who hadn't played an NHL game were signed for more money than established NHL stars. They did not automatically defer to veterans and they wore their hair as they pleased.

Mediocre players who previously would never have been able to play in the NHL now had regular jobs. Keon, and others like him, had spent years establishing their places in the pecking order, only to find the system abandoned when they reached the top. Outside the arena walls, traditional mores and ethics were under siege as never before. "What was happening was society was changing and McKenny and I were from a society that was much different than the one David came up in," said Jim Keon. "I don't know that he adapted as well as he should have. He just couldn't handle the lack of training and the lack of discipline the young players were coming into the league with. It just drove him crazy."

Despite his troubles, the 1970s brought Dave Keon's second decade of superb play. He averaged nearly 27 goals a season and continued to deliver inspired defensive work but the Leafs were beginning what would be a generation-long withering under Ballard. During Keon's captaincy, the Maple Leafs missed the playoffs twice and were eliminated in the quarter-finals four times. The only playoff victory came in 1975 when the Leafs beat the Los Angeles Kings in a best-of-three series before being pasted by the eventual Stanley Cup champion, the Philadelphia Flyers.

Ron Ellis, a one-time linemate, said the team's downward spiral pained Keon immensely.

"We're not dumb. We know when the team makes good moves and bad moves," Ellis said. "All of us were quite critical of the moves that were being made and I know he voiced that to me many times. But he played the same way, whether we were playing the Philadelphia Flyers or the St. Louis Blues. You could count on him, game in and game out."

Keon was among the Leafs' most effective players in the 1975 playoffs, but as a 35-year-old he didn't garner anything more than a token contract offer from the Leafs. He continued to be among the Leafs' best players but Ballard publicly scolded him for poor leadership and, the pot calling the kettle black, poor media relations.

Ballard's criticisms were a tip-off that he thought Keon's value to the Leafs was finished. When the Leafs didn't make a respectable contract offer, Ballard's intentions became even clearer.

The New York Islanders were looking for another veteran center to push them over the top, but the Leafs demanded a top player from their roster as well as draft picks. They wanted him gone, but not to another NHL team. Keon considered suing the Leafs for depriving him of an NHL job but he realized the battle would be costly and possibly ineffective. Instead, in August, 1975, he signed with the Minnesota Fighting Saints of the WHA.

Keon left Toronto without comment. "I can't have any regrets about leaving if I can't get a job there," he later told a writer, but that was far from the truth. Keon, one of the league's greatest players, was forced out of the NHL. While he has never publicly criticized the Leafs, the scars of his departure remain.

"I think he's still very bitter towards the Leafs," said Ron Ellis. "I think Mr. Fletcher [the current general manager] and company have done a great deal to smooth over a lot of rough edges but up until Mr. Fletcher arrived, Davey Keon didn't go to the Gardens."

When the Saints folded in March, 1976, Keon signed with the Indianapolis Racers who traded him in September, 1976, to a new version of the Fighting Saints. In January, 1977, the New England Whalers obtained Keon along with Jack Carlson, Steve Carlson and John McKenzie for Danny Arndt and future considerations.

Even as his skating slowed, Keon's game, built primarily on intelligence and instinct, remained strong. He scored over 20 goals in each of his four WHA seasons and recorded 291 points in 301 WHA games. When the NHL finally absorbed four WHA teams, including the Whalers, Keon, along with the 51-year-old Gordie Howe, was still a productive player. At 39, Keon would have been the Leafs' second-best center, behind Darryl Sittler, said Whalers' coach Don Blackburn when Hartford played Toronto the first time. "He's been our best player without a doubt this year. My problem is I'm afraid of burning him out."

Keon played in 78 of the Whalers' 80 games in 1981–82. He scored eight goals and added 11 assists. When he decided to retire, the Whalers planned a press conference but Keon refused to take part. The departure from the NHL of the last Toronto Maple Leaf to win the Stanley Cup passed by without fanfare.

In 1986, Keon was elected to the Hall of Fame, in his first year of eligibility. "They inducted Dave Keon in the NHL Hall of Fame the other night and, aside from being somewhat heavier and greyer, at 46 he hadn't changed much," wrote *Ottawa Citizen* columnist Earl McRae. "His words were few and subdued, his manner aloof, and after trading pleasantries with old compatriots, he flew back to Florida and his real estate job."

Jim Keon said age has brought more contentment for his brother. "He's 55 years of age. He's got a great sense of humor and he always has. He's interesting, he reads a lot. He's a good golfer. He brings the same discipline to golf that he always has to hockey. If he doesn't play a good round, he'll go and hit a thousand balls after."

In his own way, Dave Keon still enjoys the attention of Leaf fans. During a recent stop in Toronto, two women waited outside the men's room for his autograph and Keon was touched by the enduring loyalty of his fans.

He just doesn't want to talk. "Some of those times were very difficult," Jim Keon said. "My family's credo was always, if you can't say anything good about somebody, don't say anything at all. His silence says a lot in my mind. The fact that he won't say anything means he hasn't got anything good to say."

Clearly Keon's hard feelings about his departure have not lessened, and it isn't difficult to see why. Keon may have been the finest player to ever wear the Maple Leaf. While the Leafs could have decided that he was no longer good enough to re-sign, he deserved, at the least, recognition of his service. Instead, he was bad-mouthed by Ballard, who benefited most from the winning tradition Keon had done so much to add to.

Dave Keon's name still carries great respect in Toronto. If his captaincy was unsatisfactory, his tenure as one of the Leafs' finest players was not. What is left are the memories shared by the few people who knew Dave Keon and the hundreds of thousands of fans who thought they did.

Joe Sgro is happy to hear Keon remains well. Twenty years

after Dave Keon's departure, Sgro is among the legion who remember.

"If he'd get hurt, he'd bite his tongue," Sgro said. "Never give in, never give in. That's what I'll always remember about the man. Never give in."

CHAPTER 6

DARRYL SITTLER

CAPTAIN 1975–81

Nine years after his last NHL game, the aura of an athlete still surrounds Darryl Sittler as he slides into a booth. It's midafternoon in a roadhouse half an hour away from Brantford, Ontario. Brantford's most famous hockey alumnus is, of course, Wayne Gretzky but tonight is Darryl Sittler Night at the Brantford Smoke of the Colonial Hockey League's game. Sittler has driven the two hours from Amherst, New York, to glad-hand and sign autographs.

The Leafs list Sittler as a special consultant to general manager Cliff Fletcher. While Sittler has input on player moves, his position with the Leafs is largely public relations, usually underwritten by a separate corporate sponsor.

It is a role which suits Sittler. He is not a gregarious man but at 44 he is more handsome than ever. Sittler's build remains powerful, broad shoulders that narrow to the waist. His carriage is ramrod straight.

There is gray in his hair and the modest retreat of his hairline is becoming. Unlike so many players his age, he has his own teeth and they are straight and white.

But what is most striking about Darryl Sittler is his face.

Hockey players, virtually all hockey players, carry scars from errant slashes. Whether the scars came in defeat or victory has long since been forgotten—they testify only to battles that were fought.

Sittler's face is unlined. There is no sign that his cheekbone was smashed in his final NHL season by the Leafs' Jim Korn, no network of marks around the eyes, no apparent scars at all.

Even more remarkable is Darryl Sittler's seeming lack of psychological scars. Harold Ballard liked to tear at a player's psyche before dispatching the player himself. Dave Keon left the Leafs bitter. Talented but emotionally fragile defenseman Al Iafrate crumbled under the weight of the organization's decay and had to be shipped off to Washington before he imploded. And no player endured more than Sittler during the two-and-a-half years at the end of his 12-year career with the Leafs.

Yet Sittler is unscathed and matter-of-fact about his battles. In a business that devours marriages, Sittler and his wife Wendy have been married for 24 years.

Sittler has survived almost all of his allies and his adversaries. Alan Eagleson, the former head of the National Hockey League's Players' Association and a key Sittler supporter, has been indicted by a U.S. grand jury for racketeering, and investigations continue on both sides of the border into allegations of wrongdoing as a union executive. Eagleson faces the prospect of spending many of his remaining years in jail.

Harold Ballard died in April, 1990, a largely hated man. His children and girlfriend fought for his assets while he lay on his deathbed. The only reminder of his reign are his initials, scrawled into the concrete at center ice in the Gardens' floor and a few pictures that line the Gardens' corridors.

Two-time Maple Leafs general manager Punch Imlach, Sittler's most ferocious opponent, was harshly criticized for his treatment of Sittler and fired in 1982. He never held another job and died in December, 1987.

Gerry McNamara, the Leafs' general manager who dragged his feet and finally dealt Sittler in a desperate and one-sided trade, was fired in 1988. Nick Polano, whom Sittler openly opposed in his final year in the league, lost his job coaching the Detroit Red Wings largely, he says, because of the damage Sittler inflicted. He now heads the Calgary Flames' scouting department.

Sittler's battles were usually fought on moral grounds. When Ballard harassed Laurie Boschman over his conversion to Christianity, it was Sittler who defended the young forward. When Ballard treated Dave Keon as a has-been, it was Sittler who rebuked his employer and publicly spoke of the debt the team owed its longtime stars.

But even moral battles have more than one truth. Right and wrong, even in hindsight, isn't always clearcut.

Sittler's battles with Imlach were destructive not only to the franchise but to both men. It was Sittler who tore the C off his jersey. It was Sittler who permitted the on-ice ostracizing of Imlach retread Carl Brewer.

"The guy running the club was not his kind of guy. It was as simple as that," said writer Scott Young, a friend of both Sittler and Imlach. "With another man there, Sittler might be playing yet, he was that good. There was a destructiveness about it that did them both in."

If prosecutors who want to jail Eagleson prove their charges, Sittler will be disappointed but will remain Eagleson's friend. "I wouldn't break a friendship over that. He didn't do anything personally to me," Sittler said. "Because a guy has done something wrong, do you turf him out of your life? I think friendship is deeper than that."

Eagleson is accused of cheating the NHLPA out of hundreds

of thousands of dollars and of defrauding the most vulnerable players through career-ending insurance settlements. If Eagleson is guilty, his victims are the very people whom Sittler, a vice-president of the NHLPA, was entrusted with protecting.

In the often cartoonish world of the Maple Leafs during the 1970s and 1980s, Sittler's image was golden. His values and character were unimpeachable, especially when compared to Ballard and his management team. That image remains and for the people who respect Darryl Sittler, and they are legion, it is enough that he is loyal and that he will lead.

"What you see is what you get with Darryl," longtime linemate Lanny McDonald said. "If you go down fighting, whether it be a seventh game or with friendships, when the final buzzer goes, you know he'll still be there."

Throughout his six seasons as the captain of the Leafs, Sittler embodied the rural traditions of self-reliance and toughness.

He grew up in St. Jacobs, a small Southern Ontario farming town near Kitchener, best known as the center of a thriving Mennonite community. Ken, a crane operator, and Doris Sittler raised eight children with little money. The Sittler children learned a healthy work ethic and were often hired by local farmers.

"I worked with the Mennonite people. You were paid three bucks a day and you ate three solid meals," Sittler recalled after asking the waitress for a clubhouse sandwich and a salad. "Picking potatoes and, in the fall, picking apples, cleaning out pig manure in the barns. In a small town, the farms were only a bicycle drive away."

Darryl was a product of the 1950s. His first decent skates were Bauer Supreme hand-me-downs, once worn by former neighbor and NHLer Rod Seiling. Sittler had two pairs of pants and the same number of shirts to get him through the school week.

"We grew up in a family where we all had to work," Sittler said. "I remember paying room and board at 13 or 14. Part of the money I made had to go to the house."

By ten, Sittler was a seasoned worker. Because many Mennonites live in the area, much of the travel through St. Jacobs was, and still is, by horse and wagon. At dawn every Saturday morning, Sittler would go to work for the town, shoveling manure off the main street. He used his pay to buy hockey equipment.

St. Jacobs did not have an indoor arena so Sittler played all his minor hockey in nearby Elmira. Still, the lessons of St. Jacobs, the stubborn self-reliance that is bred into farming and rural life, carried him into the heart of urban Canada.

"I'd call Darryl a very pragmatic guy," said Jim Kernaghan, a *London Free Press* reporter who knows Sittler well and covered him as one of the hockey beat writers for the *Toronto Star*. "There's a certain Teutonic way about him. He certainly can be a stoic, he can put up with lot of pain. He's done it."

"The rural background is about knowing how hard a lot of those people had to work as a family to survive," noted McDonald, himself a native of the small town of Hanna, Alberta. "You pull your weight because you're afraid to let the rest of the family down. That's the way he played. He was always afraid that he might be the weak link.

He was anything but. Sittler led or tied for the lead in the club's scoring from 1972–73 to 1979–80 and holds ten club records, a club record in itself. He tops the Maple Leafs' list in goals (389) and points (916). Only six players, George Armstrong, Tim Horton, Borje Salming, Dave Keon, Ron Ellis and Bob Pulford, played in more games for the Leafs.

Sittler was inducted into the Hockey Hall of Fame in 1989 but the truth of Sittler's career is that he was the brightest star in a time dominated by the team's failure. He was never a first team all-star and was chosen for the second team only once. While it is true that he played at the same time as Phil Esposito and later Wayne Gretzky, it is worth noting that none of the 152 fifty-goal seasons in the NHL's history belongs to Darryl Sittler.

Aside from two remarkable games, his ten-point night on February 7, 1976, against Boston and his five-goal game in the 1976 playoff against Philadelphia, he is absent from the NHL's record book. Before the 1994–95 season, he sat 24th on the league's all-time goal-scoring ladder and 29th in points. He never won a Stanley Cup and played in the semi-final only once, captaining a Leafs' team that went down four straight to a magnificent Montreal club.

Sittler skated with a powerful but too rigid stride. He was not a particularly gifted playmaker—his passes were consistent and solid but unspectacular. His most tangible asset was a good shot but his linemate, Lanny McDonald, was among many NHLers who could shoot the puck harder.

Sittler shone because of the variety of his talents. If he wasn't the best skater, he was certainly among the league's upper half. If his shot wasn't of McDonald's caliber, it was more than respectable, and the consistency and tenacity of his play hid the fact that he lacked the imagination flashed by Wayne Gretzky or Mario Lemieux.

"He wasn't the best stickhandler in the world and he didn't have the greatest shot," said McDonald. "He wasn't the toughest guy in the league either but probably was in the top three quarters of every division. You put it all together and add a huge heart, you've got a guy you'd like to go to war with."

Sittler's package of skills was very much in keeping with the tradition of Leafs' captains. Unlike other captains, Maurice Richard or Jean Beliveau in Montreal, Esposito in Boston, Bobby Clarke in Philadelphia, Gretzky in Edmonton and Los Angeles, and Lemieux in Pittsburgh, the captain of the Toronto Maple Leafs has never been the dominant player of his era.

Only Syl Apps and perhaps Doug Gilmour were exceptionally gifted. Rick Vaive had a superb shot and an uncommon willingness to endure punishment but the rest of his game was unexceptional. Other Maple Leaf captains, from Hap Day to Ted Kennedy to Sittler, were premier character players with good skills, rather than extraordinarily gifted players blessed with character.

If Sittler wasn't the Leafs' best captain—Apps, Armstrong and Kennedy enjoyed far more team success—he was among the club's best-ever character captains. No player, not even the doggedly determined Kennedy or Armstrong, squeezed more out of their talents than Darryl Sittler did.

"When he was in a slump was when you really saw it," said Randy Carlyle, a future Norris Trophy winner who spent the first two years of his career in Toronto. "He'd stay after practice, going between the two blue lines, driving himself. I didn't notice it then but years later I appreciated how hard he worked."

That same work ethic was already evident in his early teens as Sittler set out to fashion himself into a prospect. He held down spots on bantam, midget and juvenile teams, and was chosen third overall by the London Nationals (the club changed its name to Knights in Sittler's second year) in the midget draft. The Nationals were coached by former Leafs' great Turk Broda who took both the prospect and his parents out to supper at a St. Jacobs' restaurant to seal Sittler's decision to play in London. It was Sittler's first brush with greatness and, although the old man meant little to him, Sittler was struck by the aura that surrounded even a former NHLer.

"Turk meant more to my dad than he did to me but I remember the excitement in our house when Turk was coming," Sittler said, digging into his sandwich. "Turk came and he had the fedora hat and the Camel cigarettes. He was very good to me and he was obviously a colorful character."

Broda would last only one season as coach. Sittler had no way of knowing it but his coaching carousel was just beginning. He would play for two more coaches in London and at various stages of his career in Toronto he could turn around on the bench to see John McLellan, King Clancy, Red Kelly, Roger Neilson, Floyd Smith, Punch Imlach, Dick Duff, Joe Crozier or Mike Nykoluk. In Philadelphia, Sittler played for Pat Quinn and Bob McCammon, and Nick Polano coached him in Detroit. All told, Sittler would be coached by 12 different men in the NHL. His relations with many would be difficult.

Sittler scored 76 goals and recorded 189 points in 107 junior games, positioning himself as one of the top junior prospects. In fact, the Leafs were fortunate to have Sittler to pick eighth in the 1970 draft; he should have gone to the Montreal Canadiens. Picks one through four were straightforward: Buffalo won the coin toss to choose spectacular center Gilbert Perreault. Vancouver chose the player generally conceded to be the second best that year, defenseman Dale Tallon. Boston selected Reg Leach, a prospect who would blossom into a star in Philadelphia, and the Flyers took productive forward Rick MacLeish. The Canadiens held the fifth and sixth choices, the result of a series of lopsided deals in which Montreal general manager Sam Pollock dealt discards and spare parts for first-round draft choices. Pollock was prescient in recognizing the importance of the draft but the Canadiens drafted poorly.

Using draft choices acquired from the Oakland Seals and the Minnesota North Stars, Montreal chose Ray Martiniuk, a goalie whose tour of the minor leagues eventually included Kansas City, Seattle, Oklahoma City, Baltimore, Columbus, Salt Lake City and Tucson, and Chuck Lefley, a good NHLer who played nine seasons and enjoyed a 43-goal year in St. Louis.

Hap Day and Conn Smythe shake hands at Day's wedding. Smythe used to love to tease Day about his occasional malapropisms and garnered plenty of mileage out of Day's wedding day speech that began: "Now that we have consummated the marriage." *Photo:* Courtesy of Kerry Day.

With Toronto goalie Turk Broda looking on, Syl Apps begins a charge up-ice against the Montreal Canadiens in the 1946-47 season. *Photo:* Imperial Oil-Turofsky/Hockey Hall of Fame.

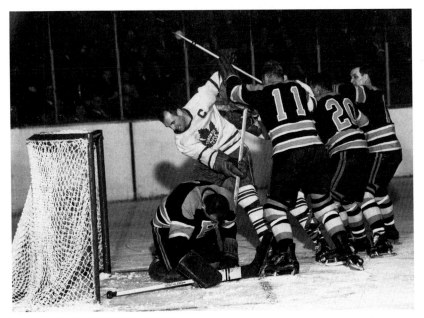

The quintessential Ted Kennedy. The Leaf captain battles a quartet of Boston Bruins as he tries to poke the puck past Boston goalie Frank Brimsek in a game at Maple Leaf Gardens in the 1954-55 season. *Photo:* Imperial Oil-Turofsky/Hockey Hall of Fame.

The great Teeder Kennedy with the 1951 Stanley Cup. Kennedy captained
the Leafs to Cups in the 1948-49 and 1950-51 seasons. *Photo:* Imperial Oil-
Turofsky/Hockey Hall of Fame.

George Armstrong, shown here as a member of the AHL Pittsburgh Hornets, was considered a can't miss prospect when he broke into the NHL but soon found himself a borderline player. He used grit and intelligence to forge a 20-year NHL career. *Photo:* Courtesy, The Hockey News.

Leafs captain George Armstrong (right) hams it up for the camera while "schooling" winger Bob Pulford. Pulford, now the general manager of the Chicago Blackhawks, was one of a score of young players Armstrong mentored.

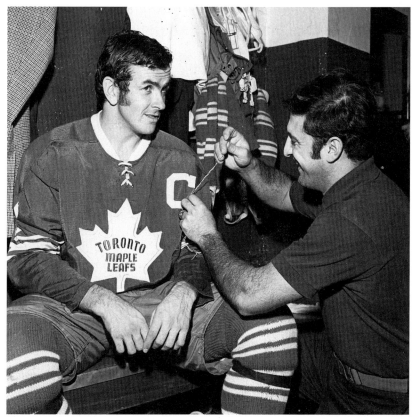

From the beginning, the C did not sit naturally on Dave Keon. For this photo, taken the day Keon assumed the captaincy, trainer Joe Sgro faked the stitching of the C to Keon's uniform. The jersey actually belonged to George Armstrong. Notice the sleeves, pinned to obscure Armstrong's number 10.

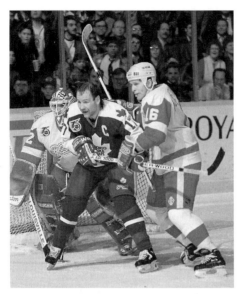

Wendel Clark battles Detroit defenseman Vladimir Konstantinov for position at the Red Wings crease during a 1993-94 season game. *Photo:* Doug MacLellan/Hockey Hall of Fame.

Dave Keon moves in on Pittsburgh Penguins goalie Andy Brown in a game at Maple Leaf Gardens in the 1970-71 season. *Photo:* Graphic Artists/Hockey Hall of Fame.

Rick Vaive had everything going for him – good looks, a great shot, a beautiful and witty wife, but his tenure in Toronto was nonetheless a long struggle. *Photo:* Miles Nadal/Hockey Hall of Fame.

With Hartford goalie John Garrett positioned behind him, Darryl Sittler readies for a scoring chance. *Photo:* Miles Nadal/Hockey Hall of Fame.

Wendel Clark catches a break and chats with an official after yet another collision. *Photo:* Doug MacLellan/Hockey Hall of Fame.

Doug Gilmour battles Mike Vernon and Nicklas Lidstrom near the Detroit cage. *Photo:* Dan Hamilton.

The Pittsburgh Penguins then took Greg Polis, a solid NHL player who would appear in more than 600 games, but, choosing eighth, the Leafs landed the steal of the first round in Darryl Sittler.

Leafs' management immediately assigned number 27 to Sittler, no small tribute since it had last been worn by superstar Frank Mahovlich. Nevertheless, Sittler, initially at least, was a bust. Because the Maple Leafs were well-stocked at center with Dave Keon, Norm Ullman, Mike Walton and Jim Harrison, Sittler was deployed on left wing. Ellis played right wing on a line usually centered by either Walton or Harrison.

The adjustment of playing out of position, along with injuries—an ankle injury in his first season and a wrist injury in his sophomore year—limited Sittler to ten- and 15-goal campaigns in his first two years. But when Harrison left for the WHA's Alberta Oilers in 1972, Sittler moved back to center. He responded with his first solid year as a pro. He more than doubled his point total by scoring 29 goals, adding 48 assists and claiming his first of eight club scoring titles.

Sittler followed up with 38- and 36-goal seasons as the good Toronto teams of the late 1970s began to take shape. Lanny McDonald's first two seasons, 1973–74 and 1974–75, were even worse than Sittler's but, by his third year, McDonald had arrived. He was playing with Sittler and ready to embark on the nine-year run that would see him total at least 30 goals a season. Gifted defenseman Borje Salming, discovered by McNamara on a scouting trip to Sweden, stepped into the NHL and quickly became an impact player. Errol Thompson, drafted by the Leafs right after Sittler, blossomed in his third season, 1974–75, and Ian Turnbull, another offensively talented defenseman, arrived to complement Salming.

The arrival of the World Hockey Association in 1972 accelerated the Leafs' player turnover. No team was slower to come to terms with the realities of a new and open marketplace than the Maple Leafs. Harrison's defection along with defensemen Rick Ley and Brad Selwood and future Hall of Fame goalie Bernie Parent stripped the team of some of its best young players in the WHA's first year of operation.

Most of the players who jumped to the WHA wanted to stay in Toronto but the Leafs' contract offers were so ludicrously low that returning to Toronto would have meant complete capitulation. Any attempt to negotiate a substantially higher wage invariably triggered public criticism by Ballard to friends in the media.

The veneer of respectability Conn Smythe had so painstakingly acquired for the Maple Leafs was cracked and peeling. Sittler's only recollection of Stafford Smythe, Smythe's son and chosen successor, was that he was almost always drunk.

The player losses finally induced the Leafs to accept the reality of a competing league and in July, 1973, Sittler used their acceptance to leverage a new contract.

The deal gave Sittler tangible proof of his value to the franchise. His salary was increased from $29,000 to $175,000 and, in a gesture of largess that would come back to haunt the Leafs' management, the club agreed to a no-trade clause in the five-year, $750,000 deal.

Sittler signed the contract while Ballard was on a weekend pass from Millhaven Penitentiary in Kingston where he was serving time for fraud and theft.

GM Jim Gregory, a soft-spoken, competent executive, was managing the Leafs, but when Ballard got out of jail he was free to meddle at will with the club's personnel decisions.

When Keon's contract expired in 1975, he was offered far less than market rate and Ballard publicly labeled him a poor leader. Although Keon was 35 and a 15-year Maple Leafs' veteran, the club essentially forced him to jump to the WHA.

For management, the immediate question was who would fill the captaincy.

The clear choice seemed to be Ron Ellis. The veteran right-winger had been groomed for the job and was the only holdover from the Leafs' 1967 Cup winner. At 30, he was the club's senior man in service and although he coveted the captaincy he told Gregory he would understand if Sittler was chosen. That's precisely what happened.

"I knew at the time that they had made the right decision," said Ellis. "Darryl had shown himself to be a great leader and he had all those years ahead of him." Ellis, a well-liked, industrious player, became one of Sittler's chief lieutenants and supporters.

When he accepted the lettered sweater from Leafs' executive Bob Davidson, Sittler was 24 and the second-youngest Leaf captain ever. Only Ted Kennedy, named captain at 22, earned the letter at a younger age. Sittler's successor, Rick Vaive, would be the youngest captain ever.

Sittler set the tone for his captaincy from the start. An hour after officially receiving the C, reporters pressed Sittler about the club's ham-handed treatment of Keon and Norm Ullman, another veteran forced out of Toronto.

"I thought the Keon and Ullman situations were handled very badly," Sittler answered. "I know Mr. Ballard is noted for being outspoken but, in this case, I thought it was dead wrong."

"The point I was making was, they were good players who gave their heart and their talents to the Maple Leafs," Sittler remembered at lunch. "Because you feel you no longer want those talents doesn't mean you have to put them down or bad-mouth them. Make a deal, fine, but acknowledge their contribution. What Harold did, there's no need for that. Davey Keon won the Lady Byng, the Calder Trophy. He was a fabulous player and his heart was with the Leafs. There was no reason for Harold to downgrade him."

Later that same day, Sittler, with ominous prescience, told a *Star* reporter, "What went through my mind is that he'll be saying the same things about me when I'm of no benefit to him anymore."

Sittler's remarks at that first press conference signaled the arrival of a new style of captain. Player acquiescence to management had been on the wane since the advent of the NHLPA and the WHA. Emboldened by these developments, players and even some management people spoke not of indentured labor but of cooperation and mutual benefit.

At the same press conference, Sittler also said, "It's no secret there's been poor communication between Red Kelly and most of the players the last two seasons. As captain, I can do something about that."

It would have been unthinkable for Kennedy or Armstrong to criticize the Maple Leafs publicly, let alone at the press conference announcing their captaincy. Members of the news media admired Sittler's candor and, to his credit, Gregory was unperturbed by Sittler's remarks.

"We wanted a captain who wasn't afraid to speak up for his teammates and who is a man respected by both players and management," Gregory told Toronto newspapers. "Sittler was the man."

Sittler also embodied some of the more traditional values. He stressed team. As the captain, Sittler always drove to the airport to welcome a player traded to the Maple Leafs. The team's social life revolved around him. When the Maple Leafs upset the New York Islanders in the 1978 playoffs, the all-night celebration, naturally enough, was at Sittler's house.

Sittler, like Apps and Kennedy, Armstrong and Day, was

defined by his competitiveness. "Darryl was a very competitive person," said McDonald. "He wouldn't stand anyone not trying to give their best. There were little short outbursts in the dressing room. Without ever naming that person it became very clear whether it was directed at a line or an individual."

Ellis thought Sittler borrowed from both Keon and George Armstrong, a retired but familiar figure around the Gardens. Keon was testy and sarcastic to his teammates but completely professional on the ice. Armstrong was an off-ice cutup who always exhibited affection and protectiveness toward young players.

"I think Darryl took the best of both those men," Ellis said. "Darryl was one of the muckrakers on the team. One of the things he was known for was coming in late in a conversation and getting the two people arguing with each other. Then he would go sit in his stall and laugh. On the ice, he had a lot of the Keon qualities. He was always one of the last guys off the ice in practice. He was very strong in his convictions, like a Dave Keon. That's why he had the problems he had—he always stood up for what was right."

Although Keon usually did little for rookies, when Sittler arrived in Toronto, the two got along. Whatever Keon's resentments, he saw in Sittler a prodigious worker. At practice, the two were almost always the first players on the ice and the last ones off.

By the mid-1970s the veterans had been purged and Sittler was the undisputed leader of the Leafs, respected both on the team and inside the game.

"I saw him the first time when he came back from the Canada Cup in 1976," said Randy Carlyle. "He came into the dressing room to say hello. It was like God walking in."

Sittler's status was not confined to players. "He carried

himself the way a Jean Beliveau did," said longtime NHL referee Bruce Hood. "If he asked you about something you were more apt to listen to him because of the kind of player he was."

Sittler was everything a captain should be. Tough and talented, he helped nurture McDonald into becoming a premier scorer.

When the New York Islanders tried to intimidate the Leafs, Sittler took on Gary Howatt, a human buzz-saw of a fighter, in a memorable tilt at the Gardens. While some teammates experienced the "Philly flu" when challenged by the brutal Philadelphia Flyers at the Spectrum, Sittler hammered anything wearing white.

He was available and open with the media and willing to do charity work. The Maple Leafs of the early 1970s were often a hard-living bunch but Sittler maintained an image as a good family man and a moderate drinker.

"At the core of Sittler was decency," said Scott Young, who covered the Leafs for the Toronto *Globe and Mail*. "I never saw anything to change my mind about that."

When Sittler did breach protocol, Conn Smythe was still around to remind him of the Maple Leafs' historic dignity. After his second season as captain, Sittler told a joke at a banquet about hockey players being like mushrooms—they were kept in the dark and surrounded by shit. Word reached Smythe who dashed off a note urging Sittler to refrain from swearing at public events. Sittler did.

On the ice, Sittler played like he was born to the C. In his first year as Captain, he bettered his previous year's point total by 20, scored 41 goals and recorded his first 100-point season.

His production continued unabated into the 1976–77 season but he slumped midway through the campaign. Before a February home game, Ballard criticized his captain in the newspapers, saying there seemed to be no line that Sittler could make effective. Sittler was put back on a line with McDonald and Errol Thompson for a February 7 game against the Bruins in Toronto. The game figured to be a rout. Boston had gone seven games without a loss while the Maple Leafs had just one victory in their past seven outings. Instead, Sittler recorded a ten-point night, garnering six goals and four assists, and the Leafs won 11–4. The ten points bettered the existing league record by two and included another feat never before performed: three goals in each of two successive periods.

The Bruins had just reacquired Gerry Cheevers from the WHA's Cleveland Crusaders but Boston coach Don Cherry decided not to use Cheevers until he had practiced himself back into shape. The incumbent goalie, Gilles Gilbert, was injured, leaving the Bruins with Dave Reece, a career minor leaguer who made his fourteenth and final NHL appearance against Sittler and the Leafs.

Sittler assisted on two goals in the first period, scored three with two assists in the second and then added a hat trick in the third. The final goal was a ricochet shot off Brad Park's skates from behind the goal line. None of Sittler's shots was unstoppable but none was transparently easy.

"It was amazing," said the Bruins' Andre Savard after the game. "It's like his shots were directed by radar."

Sittler's six goals tied a modern-era record. St. Louis Blues' center Red Berenson, who scored six in an 8–2 win over Philadelphia in 1968, is the only other post-war player to manage the feat.

Reece was sent back to the minors for good shortly afterward. In the Bruins' next game, Gerry Cheevers shut out Detroit.

"I can't explain it," Sittler said over lunch. "Every time you shot or passed it, it ended up in the net. It's a night that, almost 20 years later, people come up to me and they tell me they remember where they were that night. They still have their stubs from Maple Leaf Gardens."

Sittler was flooded with 3,500 pieces of mail. One Hamilton woman asked for Sittler's bedsheets and pillowcases "with a picture of your naked body stamped on them." Sittler sent an autographed photograph instead. Ballard presented him with a valuable tea set.

Sittler would hit the record books again with five goals against Bernie Parent and the Philadelphia Flyers in the playoffs. Only four other players, Newsy Lalonde, Rocket Richard, Reg Leach and Mario Lemieux have turned that trick.

Sittler played in his only Canada Cup tournament during the summer of 1976. The Soviets left many of their top players at home and played a disappointing series. Canada faced Czechoslovakia in the best-of-three final and won 2–0 when Sittler scored the Cup-clinching goal in a 5–4 overtime win. The next day, Ballard instructed his receptionists to answer the telephone, "Maple Leaf Gardens, home of Darryl Sittler."

"That was the only championship team I was on and the emotion of that, the intensity of the short series, it captured the emotion of the country," Sittler said. "I don't know why it happened to me but it did. It was the highlight of my career."

In 1977, Roger Neilson, a rookie coach from Peterborough, succeeded Red Kelly and the Leafs began to get serious. Neilson was a former high-school teacher, a low-key, likable man and a relentless tinkerer. While using film to scout had been around since Hap Day, Neilson was the first coach to take advantage of videotape technology to scout each opponent's most recent games. Now every team devotes money and personnel to videotape scouting.

When he was coaching junior, Neilson once pulled his goalie but told him to leave his stick lying in front of the goal line. There was, Neilson explained to the referee, no provision in the rule book prohibiting the move.

Although they sometimes clashed over Neilson's single-minded devotion to hockey above all else, Sittler and Neilson were an excellent match. Like Sittler, Neilson believed players should be included in making decisions. When Neilson asked for a players' committee, the Leafs eventually formed one that included Sittler, Ellis, Salming and Turnbull. Every element of the hockey player's existence, from travel arrangements and roommates to game strategy, was negotiated between players and coaches.

Neilson was often away scouting on Friday nights and he left Sittler in charge of practices. Together Neilson and Sittler pressed the Maple Leafs to update their fitness equipment and pushed for a technician to oversee the use of video.

It never occurred to Neilson that Sittler's control of the team's leadership was a problem. Neilson viewed it as an asset he inherited when he took the job.

"I didn't think I made any choice about that," Neilson said. "He was the captain and he did a good job. He helped me more than I helped him. He was probably the hardest-working guy on the team, and when your captain works harder than anyone else, it picks everybody up.

"I can remember one playoff series, it was in Atlanta, one of those two out of threes. The night before, we were having a meeting at the hotel and I had prepared kind of a pep talk. Just as I was getting ready to go into the room where the players were, I could hear Darryl talking. I stood outside and listened to him. Darryl was always able to say the right things at the right time. He just gave a real inspirational talk. I was ready to go out on the ice myself." The Leafs outscored Atlanta 9–5 en route to a two-game sweep.

Neilson saw in Sittler a complete player, right down to his choice of stick.

"He was great on the draw," Neilson said. "He was one of those centers who used a huge blade, as big as you could get. A lot of players sacrifice their blade for offense and for shooting. He wanted it for draws and for defensive play as well."

Roger Neilson's Maple Leafs were the best teams Darryl Sittler played for and the high-water mark of his NHL career. In 1977–78, Neilson's first season, the Leafs cut their goals against by more than half a goal per game and gained nine points in the standings.

In that year's playoffs, they pulled off a memorable seven-game upset of the New York Islanders on an overtime goal by McDonald. The Islanders had been 35 points better in the regular season and the Maple Leafs had lost Salming early in the series to an eye injury, but Neilson's team, short on talent but long on tenacity, intimidated the Islanders.

"That was a very hard-fought series," said Sittler, still pleased by the memory. "We were obviously the underdogs—the Islanders were expected to win the Cup—but ours was a team with a lot of character and a lot of chemistry, well coached by Roger Neilson. That was one of those teams, if you asked players around the league, they recognized the Leafs were a tough team to play against. We always finished our checks, we were always right in the games. I really enjoyed those two years and what we accomplished."

Despite being subsequently swept in four games by Montreal, the Leafs were sure they were only a few players away from being legitimate Stanley Cup contenders.

"We had five guys, Borje, Turnbull, Lanny, myself, and then Tiger [Williams], you could put us on the ice with anyone else in the National Hockey League," Sittler remembered. "What we lacked, when we ran into injuries, was depth like the Canadiens had."

The line of Sittler, McDonald and Williams was the team's nucleus. Sittler scored 45 goals and recorded 117 points in 1977–78; McDonald scored 47 goals and 87 points.

"We did have checking lines. Jimmy Jones, Jerry Butler and Pat Boutette, they did a good job," said Neilson. "But Sittler's line was one you could swing both ways. You could put it against the other team's top line, which you often had to do on the road, or you could use them in more of an offensive situation."

But the Leafs were clearly not in the same class as the Montreal Canadiens, expertly coached by Scotty Bowman and powered by one of the best defensive trios ever to play: Larry Robinson, Guy Lapointe and Serge Savard. Still, the Habs were nearing the end of a four-year Cup run and the identity of their heir apparent seemed very much in doubt. Would it be the Maple Leafs or the Islanders?

Neilson believes the Leafs were close.

"To be a Stanley Cup contender you've got to have the stars. Sittler, McDonald, Salming and Mike Palmateer were legitimate stars you could really rely on. Ian Turnbull had that great playoff against the Islanders and we had all kinds of toughness. We were a very tough team. We had good checkers and good experience, guys like Dan Maloney and Ronnie Ellis, top character people who could play."

In retrospect, the Maple Leafs were probably more than a couple of second-liners away from a championship-caliber team. Even if McDonald and Sittler were comparable to the Islanders' duo of Bryan Trottier and Mike Bossy, even if Neilson was the equal of Islanders' coach Al Arbour, the Maple Leafs' upset of the Islanders was just that—an upset. Turnbull peaked in that series and never developed into a fraction of the player he could have been. Neilson sensed this but was over-ruled by Ballard when he tried to trade him. The Islanders' defense, anchored by the superb Denis Potvin, was far supe-rior. The Leafs' veterans, Maloney and Ellis, were running out of steam and, while Palmateer was spectacular, Islanders' goalie Billy Smith would prove himself far sounder and more durable. But these deficits only make the Leafs' 1977–78 vic-tory all the more admirable. Unfortunately, the euphoria only lasted a few months.

The Maple Leafs had nine fewer points in Neilson's second season. Ballard, who had broken his usual pattern and hired an intelligent person from outside the organization, soon tired of Neilson and, to the horror of players and fans alike, fired him in February. But strapped for a coach (he was turned down by several people in the organization who had seen Neilson twist-ing in the wind) Ballard reinstated Neilson and tried to pres-sure him into appearing behind the bench with a paper bag over his head. Neilson refused, was rehired anyway but was quickly fired when the Leafs lost to the Canadiens in the first round in another four-game sweep.

This time, Ballard opted for a broader housecleaning, firing Jim Gregory as well. Gregory learned about his dismissal when an official from the NHL offered him a job. When he explained that he was still under contract to the Maple Leafs, the official said he had been told that Gregory was available. The official was right, and Gregory is now the vice-president for hockey operations.

If the loss of Neilson was damaging, the firing of Gregory was devastating. Gregory was the last Maple Leafs' GM with the expertise and the patience to manipulate Ballard. "As soon as I saw Jim Gregory was gone, I knew the Leafs were in big trouble," Neilson said.

Ballard's bunker buddy, King Clancy, talked up Punch Imlach, who had been let go as Buffalo's general manager the previous year, as the best man for the Leafs' vacant GM job. Imlach had done a wonderful job with the Sabres, turning them from expansion doormats into Stanley Cup finalists within five years. But his autocratic methods eventually distanced him from many of his players, his hand-picked coaches, Joe Crozier, Floyd Smith and Marcel Pronovost, and the club's owners, Seymour and Northrup Knox. Once, when the Knoxes insisted against Imlach's wishes on playing an exhibition game against a touring Soviet team, he booked the Buffalo Auditorium from under the owners' noses and refused to surrender the ice.

After eight years, he was fired on December 4, 1978. The Sabres have yet to appear in another Stanley Cup final. Imlach, who enjoyed a spectacular four Stanley Cup-run as the Leafs' coach in the late 1950s and early 1960s was announced as the Leafs' latest GM on July 4, 1979. It was Independence Day in the United States. The fireworks would start soon enough in Canada.

Where Sittler saw a promising team, loaded with character, Imlach saw a slow, untalented, undisciplined team run not by a coach but by a player: Darryl Sittler. In his book, *Heaven and Hell in the NHL*, Imlach summed up the Leafs and Sittler this way: "They were a close-knit group with Sittler as leader. He hadn't led them anywhere, but nobody seemed to realize that. He was the focal point and the players practically ran their own show. If they'd been contenders, being close-knit would have been great. But they were a solid ninth-place team made up mainly of plodders and grinders, not skaters."

Conn Smythe, in his autobiography, *If You Can't Beat 'Em in the Alley*, described Imlach as the best coach and the worst general manager he had ever known. "I was never in his class as a coach," Smythe wrote in 1980. "However, as a general manager, I never lost a good player because I couldn't get along with him, and Imlach did." Smythe was referring specifically to Frank Mahovlich but his words describe the Punch Imlach who would soon do battle against Darryl Sittler, his most valuable player.

The temptation when describing the Sittler-Imlach wars is to cast Imlach as evil incarnate and Sittler as the sole person with integrity in a morally bankrupt organization. But, in retrospect, Imlach was correct that the Maple Leafs weren't good enough to win the Stanley Cup. The problem was that they would become far worse, first under Imlach and later under a succession of coaches and general managers.

By the time he arrived for his second Toronto stint, Imlach's courage and grit had calcified into destructive tunnel vision. Anger over the relish Stafford Smythe seemed to have taken in firing him after the Leafs were eliminated from the 1969 playoffs had never left Imlach. A decade after the firing, writing about it in his second autobiography, Imlach's vitriol remained undiluted.

He was, Imlach said, "fired the way a foreman cuts a casual laborer who's been leaning too much on his shovel."

Imlach arrived in Toronto a man out of step with his time.

In 1958, Imlach's first year in Toronto, teams played 70 games a season, the NHL was a six-team league and winning the Stanley Cup meant surviving only two playoff series. The owners had crushed an early players' association and enjoyed a disproportionate amount of power. Conn Smythe once traded a player for marrying during the regular season against his orders—near-total control over players was the norm.

But then came the WHA and the union. The WHA not only blew the lid off salaries, it gave players a legitimate voice in their future and agents an entry into the league's power structure that they have never relinquished. Nevertheless, as late as 1971 Imlach refused to deal directly with agents.

What undermined Imlach in both Buffalo and Toronto was an absolute refusal to accept the erosion of management's power and an unwillingness to alter what had been a winning formula in his earlier term with the Maple Leafs. Imlach's problem wasn't so much Sittler (in fact, Ballard's destructive meddling was the franchise's greatest millstone) as his own hostility to change.

"I recognize that I am a stubborn, tough bastard to deal with, but that's why I've been successful, so why change it?" Imlach wrote in *Heaven and Hell in the NHL.* "If that makes me unacceptable to the chronic losers, so be it."

Of all the changes Imlach failed to understand, the most important for the Leafs and Sittler was the evolution of the captain's role.

Captains had traditionally been expected to lead only where the organization saw fit. Sittler saw his role as leading the players, not for management's benefit, but for the common good. He refused to surrender to Imlach the influence and power he had acquired. Confrontation was inevitable.

"The captain is a player," Sittler said over lunch. "It's important for management to have strong communication and a relationship with the captain and assistant captains so you understand each other's thoughts and differences. That way, you're both in it for the common goal to be successful. Imlach, all the time, was I and You. I couldn't understand why he couldn't see. I'd even talk to him; I'd say times are different from the forties and fifties and sixties. Communication is important now. If we're going to be successful it's going to have to be this way."

"At the core of Imlach there was a tremendous competitiveness and belief in himself," said Scott Young. "As time went on, this became bitterness. Imlach had won four Stanley Cups. He thought, quite properly, he had some idea how to run a hockey team that would win Stanley Cups. The way you would argue against Sittler, and Imlach did, was, 'What the hell do you mean you've got a great hockey team? You've never been better than seventh or eighth place and it's going in the same direction again.' "

Imlach felt Sittler, at 29, had already lost a step. Where Neilson saw a selfless player, Imlach believed Sittler was selfish and mediocre defensively.

"And Sittler's image was also one of loyalty," Imlach wrote. "I rather envied that. I wished he could have been loyal to me in my attempts to make the team better, or to Harold Ballard, or to the general good of the Leafs, rather than to the NHL Players' Association, Alan Eagleson, and to those Leaf players who never, in a million years, were going to win the Stanley Cup."

Gord Stellick, the Leafs' radio color commentator who was then Imlach's assistant, said that while Imlach was warm to those who worked for him, his decisions were driven by ego.

"The moment he arrived, he wanted to get his own Gil Perreault and build them up like he had in Buffalo. If they won with Borje Salming, Darryl Sittler, Mike Palmateer and Ian Turnbull, that was no good. Right off the bat, before they dropped the puck, he took issue with the captain who he felt was more of a shop steward than a captain."

The first confrontation, fittingly enough, was over a television intermission feature called *Showdown*. This program was an NHL-NHLPA promotional package that matched players in testing skills and taking penalty shots.

Imlach didn't like the event because he worried that participating players would be injured. Borje Salming had broken his finger in 1978 while taping the program and missed both the preseason and training camp. Detroit goalie Rogie Vachon also injured a knee in the event. In Buffalo, Imlach pressured Danny Gare and Gilbert Perreault into not participating and he tried to do the same thing with the Leafs' representatives, Mike Palmateer and Darryl Sittler.

The first real conversation between Sittler and Imlach was an argument in Imlach's office in late August over the event. Imlach ordered Sittler not to go and said he had decided to send Paul Gardner instead. It was, Sittler recalled, not a request. "That's his personality, that's how he managed, with confrontation and fear," Sittler remembered. "To me that sums it up. He was always willing or eager to test the limit. He would try to test the character of the person to see if they would stand up to him."

By now, Sittler was the vice-president of the NHLPA and he had no intention of reneging on his commitment to *Showdown*. Imlach and Ballard tried to obtain a court injunction preventing Sittler and Palmateer's participation but failed, and they competed as scheduled. It was a poor beginning and the tension invariably escalated.

As surely as Imlach was driven to cut Sittler down to size, Sittler was determined not to surrender the heart of the team to Imlach or his coaches, Floyd Smith and Joe Crozier, whom he viewed as Imlach's lackeys.

"There was never any question Sittler could lead," Scott Young said. "He led that team away from Punch Imlach about as far as it could go." Sittler fought Imlach deliberately, patiently, perhaps even ruthlessly.

"Sittler very coldly sized up the situation and said Imlach is wrong on how he's handling the team and this can't continue," remembered Jim Kernaghan. "He wasn't screaming or hollering."

The Leafs surrendered nearly a goal a game more in 1979–80 than in the previous season under Neilson and were brushed aside by Minnesota in three straight games in the first round of the playoffs.

That summer, Ballard said Sittler was a cancer to the Maple Leafs. The public defrocking of a Toronto Maple Leafs' captain was underway.

Imlach knew Sittler would never relinquish his leadership. But when he tried to trade him, he found the no-trade clause in Sittler's contract.

To Sittler, accepting a trade would have been to surrender. "Why would I?" he said over lunch. "I had a no-trade contract. I was popular with my teammates. I was popular with the media, the fans."

Early in Imlach's first season, he had forbidden Sittler to appear on *Hockey Night in Canada*. He asked Sittler to resign as vice-president of the NHLPA and to ditch Eagleson, who Imlach hated, as his agent. Sittler discussed the team on the radio instead and kept Eagleson.

Imlach brought back an over-the-hill Carl Brewer and got rid of Dave Hutchison, one of Sittler's better friends. The players ostracized Brewer and routinely refused to pass to him, a choice Sittler refused to censure. This behavior incensed Imlach even more.

In 1979, Imlach put the entire team on recallable waivers. But it was in December of that year that the single most damaging incident occurred between Sittler and Ballard.

Ballard, without the approval of the NHLPA, scheduled an exhibition game between the Leafs and the Canadian Olympic team and then called a press conference to publicize his generosity. The event, to be played February 6 during a heavy leg of the schedule, was a fund-raiser for Ronald McDonald House, a charity that listed Sittler as its honorary chairman.

Before the press conference, the players held a meeting of their own, organized by Sittler and Eagleson, in which they voted overwhelmingly not to play the game. The players said they would relent only if they were given the chance to face a touring Soviet team, a surefire stab at Ballard who hated the Soviets and refused to allow them in the Gardens. They also stipulated that the game against the Canadian Olympians would be a lighthearted affair in which the goaltenders and several players would swap sides. "It wouldn't draw flies," Imlach commented.

Sittler and Ron Ellis were the only players who voted to play the game. Nonetheless, Sittler and Eagleson walked into the middle of Ballard's press conference.

"Now I'm the spokesperson. I walk into the press conference and Harold had no idea," Sittler said. "I announced we weren't going to play. Harold was floored, like I was grandstanding. But I was in a position of responsibility. We had a vote. I wanted to play the game and go ahead with it but the headlines in the paper were like it was my battle against Imlach or my battle against Harold. I was the victim of circumstances."

Ballard was furious and Imlach moved quickly. The no-trade clause meant he could not trade Sittler without his permission but he could certainly make life hellish for him by getting rid of his supporters.

First, he traded Pat Boutette, a gritty, industrious player, to Hartford for a career minor leaguer named Bob Stephenson. Next, Imlach traded Lanny McDonald, Sittler's closest friend, and defenseman Joel Quenneville to the Colorado Rockies for Pat Hickey and Wilf Paiement.

"Sure McDonald can score, but Paiement can do more things for you than McDonald," Imlach told Ballard. "Hickey has one 40-goal season behind him. Quenneville, I feel we can let him go."

Paiement was a good player who enjoyed a 40-goal year the following season but Hickey's career was in free-fall. It was a ludicrous deal, one Imlach's detractors were sure he had fashioned only to rid the team of McDonald.

What Imlach did wasn't new to the league. Twenty years before, Detroit Red Wings' general manager Jack Adams tired of the influence and union activities of his 32-year-old captain Ted Lindsay and traded him to Chicago. Adams re-established his authority but at a terrible cost. The Red Wings, four-time Stanley Cup winners with Lindsay, never won another Cup. Imlach couldn't trade Sittler but he could and did damage him.

Imlach had gutted the Leafs for no positive result. Stephenson played 14 games. Within three seasons, both Paiement and Hickey were dealt away. Palmateer was soon dispatched and it took ten years for the Maple Leafs to land a better goalie in Felix Potvin. Imlach did make one good deal, acquiring Rick Vaive and Bill Derlago for Tiger Williams and Jerry Butler, but, on balance, the moves were devastating, not only to the level of talent but to the direction of the franchise.

"All the years I played, I knew at training camp if we had a chance," Ellis said. "I knew that team had a chance. So did Darryl, so did McDonald, so did Salming and everybody else that was there. We knew we were good, two or three players away from possibly a Stanley Cup run. If we knew, management must have known it and the question was, why did it have to happen?"

"The point is not whether you were going to win the Cup with that team," Sittler said. "The point was whether you were going to be competitive. What happened after those trades, the Leafs went right down to the bottom. The deals that he made were bad deals."

Sittler would not quit the Leafs, but he had had enough of the captaincy. On December 30, 1979, the day after McDonald was traded, Sittler drafted a letter to the media on his own stationery, skated in the pregame warmup before a game against Winnipeg, took off his jersey and then retreated to a toilet stall in the rear of the Leafs' dressing room.

"I had jotted down a number of points because I knew it would be a media circus after the game," Sittler said. "Nobody knew, just my wife. I came off early in warmups and asked the trainer [Guy Kinnear] for a scalpel. It was triple stitched. I was nervous. 'Guy,' I said, 'Don't ask any questions. Can you do this for me?' Then I went and talked to my teammates. It was a very emotional speech."

Tiger Williams tried to talk Sittler out of quitting but Sittler refused. After an initial delay because the ice-surfacing machine had broken down, Sittler returned to the ice. For the first time in more than four years, he was not wearing the C.

"That was a very difficult and very emotional thing," Sittler said. "I didn't do it in the essence or the mood of a spoiled brat, or I'm going to get even. I thought about it a lot before the Lanny trade.

"When I decided to take off the C, I said to myself, 'Why am I here? All this other crap is going on around me. I'm here because I love playing hockey; I love being successful on the ice.' Imlach really didn't want me to be his captain. My battles became the focal point of the team. All I was doing was sticking up for myself. Finally I said, 'Take the C off. Be a player. You're getting well paid and people want to see you play; your teammates do too. Just remove that responsibility.'

"That's why I did it. I explained it to my teammates, the coaches, and went out and played."

Williams took on the role of acting captain. Sittler had an assist, and the Leafs beat Winnipeg 6–1 before the ex-captain ducked out the back door to avoid reporters.

Tearing off the C was as dramatic as it was unprecedented but the media was largely sympathetic to Sittler.

Imlach, meanwhile, responded curiously. He tried to get
Sittler to leave town, even offering him a free trip to Florida.

Sittler remembered how Imlach had pressured Frank
Mahovlich during his later years into leaving the club and then
implied he had suffered a nervous breakdown. Hockey was
about playing and Sittler would play.

Remarkably, Sittler finished the year with 43 goals and 96
points but there would be no first-round upset of the Islanders.
In a fitting demonstration of the damage Imlach had wrought,
the North Stars swept the Leafs 3–0 and outscored them 19–8.
Ballard said his ex-captain would not be back. He even went to
the trouble of scratching Sittler's name from the players invited
to training camp. Sittler attended anyway.

But while Ballard publicly backed his general manager, he
was privately shocked at the support, among both fans and
media, for Sittler. The McDonald trade had generated actual
fan protests and the spectacle of a few spectators attending
games with paper bags on their heads drove home the unpopu-
larity of Imlach's decisions.

Besides, Ballard was notoriously fickle. Sittler had been care-
ful never to slam Ballard in the media and Ballard had a remarkable capacity to be influenced by the last person he spoke to.

Sittler sensed a chance for peace. He asked Imlach to
arrange a meeting with Ballard. Imlach, believing the meeting
would be the prelude to Sittler's departure, agreed.

That August, just days before the meeting, Imlach suffered
his third heart attack. Imlach's hospitalization made him irre-
sistibly easy to ignore. Sittler and Ballard struck what would
be a temporary truce and Sittler agreed to take the C back.

"I could always sense that Harold was uncomfortable with
what was happening but he didn't come forward and say anything," Sittler recalled. "After Punch had a heart attack, he
specifically told me then, Punch will not be back. He said he

had made a mistake in hiring him and he had destroyed what we had going."

Imlach got a get-well card from Sittler but not so much as a note from Ballard. When Imlach came back in mid-November, Ballard told him it was too dangerous for him to work and kept Gerry McNamara on as acting general manager. Imlach never worked in the NHL again.

Sittler had outlasted Imlach, but the tumult of the Gardens showed no sign of abating. McNamara, who had been pulled from the player evaluation ranks, was abrupt and often unreadable but Ballard liked him because he defended him to the media and did as he was told.

Ballard fed on that lack of resistance and steadily grew more outrageous and covetous of publicity.

In the fall of 1981, Sittler approached Ballard about money. He would turn 31 during the season and was in the sixth year of a seven-year contract extension. In the contract's final year, Sittler was scheduled to make $190,000 plus bonuses. Although the long-term deal had brought security, by the end of the contract, Sittler was being paid well below market value. Salming was making over $300,000 and Paiement and Hickey were also outdrawing Sittler at the pay window. Sittler based his request on two milestones he was approaching—one thousand games as a Maple Leaf and one thousand points.

"I went in to Harold and I said, 'Listen. I'm not coming here for a new contract. I realize you've signed other players, I realize I still have a couple of years left on my contract. I'd like you to consider, when I score my thousandth point or play my thousandth game as a Leaf, that you might do something in a bonus for that.' He said, 'Hey, no problem. I've got to go to the board of directors and talk about it'."

Ballard was lying. The move was a dodge. He needed no authority from the board.

Sittler waited until after the board meeting that November to contact Ballard. He phoned from Ian Turnbull's pub to set up an appointment.

"The secretary put me right through to Harold and I said, 'Mr. Ballard, it's Darryl Sittler. Can I come over to see you?' And then the answer, you know how only Harold could do it in his rough, gruff voice, was, 'Darryl, we had the board of directors' meeting. There's nothing we can do for you but I'll tell you what. We'll trade you to whatever city you want to go to'."

Those words severed any remaining attachment to the Maple Leafs. "It caught me right off guard," Sittler said. "You know sometimes how that cold feeling goes through you? I said, 'If after 11 years that's how you do things, over the phone, I'll be right over.' Bang, I hung up the phone. Didn't go back to the table. I went right over to the Gardens."

Sittler demanded an instant trade but agreed with McNamara and Ballard to keep the move quiet so the club could maximize its offers. The agreement lasted a few weeks but, when word reached Sittler that Ballard was telling reporters he had duped Sittler into thinking he would be quietly traded, the affair went public.

The media now knew the Leafs were either auctioning their best player or stringing him along. Either way, it made for sensational copy.

November ran into December. By then Sittler had given to McNamara a list of teams he would consider accepting. They ranged from the Philadelphia Flyers and Minnesota North Stars, two teams with Stanley Cup potential who were hungry for a veteran center, to the New York Islanders and Buffalo Sabres. Buffalo offered Rick Martin and Chicago dangled young defenseman Doug Wilson, a future Norris Trophy winner.

Eagleson went on *Hockey Night In Canada* to say that Sittler might have played his last game. Still, McNamara couldn't strike a deal.

Then a new element entered the picture. Sittler met with club doctors who said he was suffering from exhaustion. A second doctor agreed and, when the Leafs headed to Minnesota on January 5, 1982, Sittler, citing emotional exhaustion, stayed home.

His final days as a Leaf were played out in a blaze of publicity. "Everything went wacko. I'm not in Minnesota and all the sportswriters are clustered around the house. I'm not taking any phone calls; there are threats from reporters to my wife that if you don't get him on the line, we'll do this and that."

Sittler found time to make a commercial for a local car outlet that played on the theme of a trade-in, but the final days of waiting were excruciating. A SWAT team of reporters waited outside Sittler's Mississauga home. Finally, on January 20, McNamara called Sittler at 2 a.m. from the general managers' meeting in Florida to tell him he had been traded to Philadelphia.

Even if Sittler's game was in decline, the deal was one-sided. The Leafs acquired Rich Costello, whom they described as a young Bobby Carpenter, the Flyers' second-round choice in the 1982 entry draft, who turned out to be Peter Ihnacak, and future considerations. Costello played two games with the Leafs. Ihnacak scored 102 goals over eight seasons. And the Maple Leafs filled Darryl Sittler's place on the roster with Normand Aubin.

"We took the best deal available and got something that will help us in the future," McNamara rationalized at the time. "The fact that we were stuck with someone who didn't want to play for us anymore puts us ahead of the game with this deal."

Sittler had his escape and increased financial security. In

addition to tax advantages, the move brought an immediate raise from $185,000 to $230,000 and another year on his contract. He struggled to find his bearings in Philadelphia but eventually scored 14 goals in 35 games and three more times in a four-game playoff loss to the New York Rangers.

Sittler rebounded in 1982–83 and netted 83 points in the regular season, but he played poorly as the Flyers were eliminated in three straight games, again by the New York Rangers. The loss was the most devastating in franchise history as the Flyers had been 26 points better than the Rangers in the regular season.

Sittler's goal total slipped to 27 during the 1983–84 season and again the playoffs were a disappointment. By now, coach Bob McCammon was restricting Sittler's ice time and he was one of three veterans ordered to go south for a late-season rest. This time, he did not refuse, but the trip did nothing to prevent another sweep, this one by the Washington Capitals.

The Flyers had little veteran leadership. During the summer of 1984, Bobby Clarke had retired to take over as the club's general manager. Shortly afterwards, Sittler and his former teammate met to talk contract.

Sittler was going into his option year, which meant that the following year he could sign with another team with no compensation to the Flyers. Sittler said Clarke offered him the captaincy and $100,000 in five installments on top of his $250,000 salary to re-sign with the Flyers. Sittler said he also received assurances that a job in the organization awaited him on his retirement. He took the deal.

At the end of training camp, Sittler and his teammates attended a chamber of commerce "Meet the Flyers" event in downtown Philadelphia. The event was to showcase the new team and, not incidentally, the new captain.

Sittler accepted congratulations all around and did several media interviews speaking as the Flyers' captain.

But there was no mention of the captaincy during the luncheon and the team was bussed back to the Flyers' practice arena. There, Sittler was escorted to the office of Mike Keenan, the Flyers' new coach. An ashen-faced Bobby Clarke was waiting for him.

"I walk into the office and there's Bobby Clarke and he says, 'I just traded you to Detroit.' He said, 'It was one of those deals, we were looking at younger players. You'll like it.'"

In fact, for the Flyers, it was an excellent deal. The Flyers, who were short on left wing, acquired Murray Craven, a very productive two-way player, and Joe Paterson, who potted several big goals for Philadelphia in the post-season. But for Sittler, it was a bitter irony; by signing the new contract, he had relinquished control of his destiny, a destiny he had fought so hard to shape in Toronto.

Clarke tells a different story. It was Sittler, Clarke said, who demanded the $100,000 payment to stay clear of free-agency. That demand, in Clarke's mind, wiped away any tacit understanding between the Flyers and Sittler on his future.

"Look, I know I'm not lily-white on this, but Darryl squeezed $100,000 out of me," Clarke said. "I said if we're going to be mercenary about this, all bets are off. We did the deal because I didn't think we owed Darryl anything. The deal was, absolutely, the best thing for the hockey club."

Clarke was dead right. The deal was, in fact, very good for the Flyers. The team crystallized under Keenan and advanced to the Stanley Cup final, when they lost to the Edmonton Oilers.

"Clarke thought Darryl was a better all-around player than he was," said a source close to the Flyers' GM. "Everyone was surprised that Darryl was basically a shooter. Everyone thought of him as a slightly junior grade Clarke as an all-around player but he wasn't very good defensively and he was sort of a one-dimensional guy."

"We should have protected ourselves," Sittler says now, "and put a no-trade clause in that deal. But the thrust of the negotiations was such that why would you worry about being traded?"

Despite Sittler's vehement objections, neither team would be browbeaten into canceling the deal. Sittler finally agreed to report to Detroit for the additional year on his contract but, from beginning to end, the move was a mistake.

The Red Wings were in turmoil, an old, directionless team. Red Wings' coach Nick Polano thought Sittler was washed up and had worked hard to talk general manager Jim Devellano out of the deal.

"The more I tried to play him, the more I realized it was over," Polano said. "He couldn't penetrate, he couldn't go by anybody. I couldn't use him and he would come into my office yelling and screaming, asking why I wasn't playing him."

In Sittler's first game in Toronto with the Red Wings, October 24, 1984, defenseman Jim Korn knocked him into the boards, breaking his upper cheekbone and the bone around his eye. After X-rays, Sittler walked into the emergency room at Wellesley Hospital to see his father. Ken Sittler had suffered a heart attack at the game and the same ambulance that had rushed the son to the hospital returned to the Gardens and ferried back his father. Sittler missed three weeks of action. Ken initially recovered but died of another attack in his sleep on February 6, 1985.

When Sittler and Polano met to explain why Sittler wasn't going to play on back-to-back nights, a discussion that began cordially deteriorated when Polano said Sittler's conditioning was poor.

The remark upset Sittler because it struck at the heart of his professional self-image—his work ethic. He stormed out of the coach's office. This confrontation was layered on top of another dispute. Earlier in the season, Polano had asked about practice techniques in Philadelphia and Sittler used the question to criticize Polano's practices.

Professional sport is not a democracy, although, invariably, the greater a player's productivity, the greater latitude he enjoys in criticizing management. But Sittler was, in his coach's estimation, a marginal NHLer.

"What it came down to," Polano said, "was he had to be a good guy. We didn't want him complaining to the media, trying to cause problems. He said I couldn't communicate. Communication with Darryl Sittler is giving him what he wants. He was not a good team player."

Sittler either did not dress or languished at the end of the bench for most of the season. He finished with 11 goals and 16 assists in 61 games. In the Wings' final playoff game, a loss to Chicago, Sittler wore a suit.

Sittler sees nothing wrong with confronting Polano.

"It wasn't a mistake. In my mind it wasn't. He sat me down and questioned my conditioning, which I was very proud of. If you looked at the charts at the Flyers' camp, I was 34 years old and third highest in cardiovascular condition."

Sittler wrote a letter to the Red Wings' owner, Mike Ilitch, outlining his views on the team's problems. There was no interest in Sittler on the trade market, and the Wings, wanting a fresh start, bought out Sittler's contract and didn't re-sign Polano. "Darryl Sittler," said Devellano, "was one of my biggest disappointments. Doing well himself was more important than winning. He was really an 'I' guy."

The Vancouver Canucks offered a tryout but Sittler declined.

"It wasn't an easy decision. I was going through some personal problems; it was a tough year. My wife and I were going through some of the troubles married people go through. My family had moved from Toronto to Philly to Detroit. There was no guarantee I could pick it up in Vancouver. Finally I said, I've got to do what's right for my family and career."

In the summer of 1985, Darryl Sittler retired.

It has been a busy retirement. Sittler moved into public relations, doing public speaking for Labatt's Olympic Program and Purolator Couriers, and appeared in an instructional hockey video, *One on One with the Stars*.

The first summer after his retirement, Sittler re-embraced Christianity and, with extensive counseling, he and Wendy saved their marriage. In 1987, while reading a story on skin cancer in the *Toronto Star*, Sittler remembered a mole on his shoulder. He had the growth examined and it was found to be malignant. Two small surgeries removed the cancer and it has not recurred.

In 1989, he spoke to the Maple Leafs about working in management. Gord Stellick had suggested Sittler for a job with the front office but, when Stellick quit the Maple Leafs for a job as assistant GM with the New York Rangers, the possibility disappeared.

Harold Ballard died April 11, 1990, and reporters who called Sittler expecting vitriol got instead words of sadness, even loss.

"Towards the end, I viewed him with sympathy," Sittler said. "To see how the family issue became the headlines in the papers, the feuds with his kids. I looked at him at times as a lonely man but a good person.

"I think with Harold, because of his personality, the media loved to feed off him and he loved it as much as they did. A lot of times, I would read things and take them with a grain of salt. It does have an impact what is being printed or said but, if you knew the other side of Harold, you knew sometimes he was saying it with a grain of salt or to get a reaction."

When Cliff Fletcher was brought in as GM in July, 1991, he quickly decided that a lack of tradition was an organizational weakness. One of his first moves was to hire Sittler as a special consultant.

From shoveling frozen manure as a ten-year-old to his relationships with management as a player, Darryl Sittler has never taken the expedient way. This is not to say he is selfless. Captaining the Toronto Maple Leafs was a lucrative venture that he continues to profit from, even at the Brantford Smoke's Darryl Sittler night.

In the end, Imlach was right. Darryl Sittler didn't lead the Leafs to the promised land of a Stanley Cup final. No one could. But, in his own stubborn, implacable way, Darryl Sittler tried.

"I don't think you'd ever get Darryl to say he was disappointed with the way his career went," Lanny McDonald said. "He lived a life, especially in hockey, the way he wanted to. There were times in his life where he stood up and got moved to another city, but he was still his own man and his own boss."

Buck O'Neil was an excellent baseball player in the Negro leagues who came along too early for integration and never played in the white majors. Of baseball, Buck O'Neil once wrote: "It's as good as sex; it's as good as music. It fills you up. Waste no tears for me. I didn't come along too early. I was right on time."

Darryl Sittler, the brightest star in the Toronto Maple Leafs' darkest days, says he too came along right on time.

"The reality of it is, I was fortunate to play 15 years, making a living at something I really loved doing. Had I played on another team through that period of time and did the same things on the ice, the impact and the career I left behind wouldn't have been as noticed as it was for me with the Leafs.

"To end up in the Hall of Fame, to score the winning goal at the Canada Cup and all those other things that happened... even though we didn't win the Cup," said Darryl Sittler, "I appreciated that."

CHAPTER 7

RICK VAIVE

CAPTAIN 1981–86

For no definitive reason but a dozen acceptable ones, the coach of the South Carolina Stingrays is in a bad mood.

His team isn't playing well and all the details and annoyances of life, as a husband and father in general and as a coach in the East Coast Hockey League in particular, are bubbling to the surface. So Rick Vaive goes to the North Charleston Coliseum, slips on his skates and heads for the ice with a bucket of pucks.

WHAP. A shot rockets into the net, followed by another, then another and another. Impatience, frustration, rage crystallize into a short, violent backswing and follow-through. Vaive shoots a hundred pucks. Then he shoots a hundred more, and another hundred.

Sometimes, when the pressure built up in Toronto, Rick Vaive would head out early for practice and perform this same private ritual before 15,000 empty seats. Just himself and the game broken down to its essentials: ice, puck, stick. No prattling owner, no demanding coaches, no media to placate, no ill-fitting role to bear.

"I used to love doing that, 20 minutes, 25 minutes before

practice," Vaive said in a long-distance call from Charleston. "A big pail of pucks, just me and a nice fresh sheet of ice. Skate around and shoot. It was peaceful. It was just me and the pucks and the sound."

By the time the Stingrays drift onto the ice, the coach is glistening with sweat...and smiling. "After that," he said, "all was right with the world."

Rick Vaive is 36 now and it has been 15 years since he first pulled on a Maple Leafs' sweater. His hair is mostly gray but he is in good shape, about ten pounds over his playing weight of 198. He doesn't perform this prepractice ritual very often, but then he doesn't need to. Vaive has achieved in the hockey backwater of South Carolina what he could rarely find in Toronto: contentment.

"All of us are really happy because of where Rick is at right now," said Joyce Vaive, his wife of 14 years. "He's doing what he wants to do and he's in a corner of the world that he's happy with. We've been together since we were 15 years old and this is probably the most relaxed we've been."

"I wouldn't have changed any of the years in Toronto for anything," Vaive said. "It was obviously tough but you can't help thinking that, by having that experience and by going through that, it makes you a better and a tougher person. But I just feel so much more at peace with myself right now than I did back then."

As a Maple Leafs' captain, Vaive's leadership skills never matched his talent. But as age diluted his physical gifts, his leadership qualities developed. While playing with the American Hockey League's Rochester Americans, one of his final professional stops before retirement, Vaive found players receptive, even eager to listen, when he spoke about the NHL.

The East Coast Hockey League is built on the ambition, usually misplaced, of young and marginal players. A salary cap and a limit on the number of veterans ensures youth and turnover. His players are at the lowest level of NHL affiliation; they are desperate to learn and Rick Vaive is equally willing to teach.

"It's different here. You're not dealing with egos and multi-million dollar hockey players. The kids are playing because they want to play hockey. They have good attitudes."

Vaive's life is balanced. He coaches baseball in the summer, plays recreational hockey and has both his sons in a hockey league. Golf, another passion, is available year-round. Joyce loves the area and the ocean is only a ten-minute car ride away. But Vaive overcame the final barrier to contentment when he decided to stop drinking. In March, 1994, the day after the Stingrays were eliminated from the playoffs by John Brophy's Hampton Roads Admirals, Vaive went on a bender.

Vaive has always had a low tolerance for alcohol. Six beers is enough to send him flying. He was never violent or abusive when drunk—far from it. Instead, alcohol gave him the license to shed his inhibitions.

But this time, when Vaive woke up he saw a pattern of drinking that he feared would ruin his life.

He went to a half a dozen counseling sessions and realized that, while he didn't need to drink constantly, he almost never drank moderately.

"My problem wasn't that I drank all the time. I didn't. But when I did, some nights, I couldn't stop. I had a couple of experiences last year where I'd go out and I'd intend to have three or four beers. The next thing I would know, it was three o'clock in the morning and I'm still going. Finally, I said, this isn't worth it. If I can't go out and have two or three beers and stop, I may as well not drink at all."

His marriage, Vaive said, has benefited from his decision. "I think all Joyce really wanted was for me to succeed and when she saw me on those nights I wouldn't stop, it really hurt her.

I can understand that. It took me a long time to realize that but, hey, 34 years old is better than waiting until you're in your coffin. I'm just happy it happened. I'll tell you what, our relationship is an awful lot better since last March."

Alcohol played a part in the incident that symbolized Vaive's time with the Maple Leafs; the night before he lost his captaincy for missing a practice, he had been drinking with longtime teammate John Anderson. Vaive had been in bed only a couple of hours when roommate Greg Terrion tried to wake him before heading out. Vaive rolled over, said he would get up and went back to sleep. From the moment he woke up until he left Toronto, things were never the same for Rick Vaive.

Vaive's demotion may have been the lowest point of a once-proud institution. By the early eighties, the captaincy of the Toronto Maple Leafs, once the podium for some of the game's greatest stars, was, like the franchise itself, a tired, stale shadow of its former self.

"With the Leafs," wrote Milt Dunnell when Vaive's title was stripped, "it [the C] has become more of a joke than a badge of prestige."

But even before he lost the captaincy, Vaive's time in Toronto had been difficult. There is a bittersweet lesson of life, experienced by athletes and achievers in all areas. Meeting even the most desired career goals does not guarantee happiness. Invariably, achievers discover the flaws that burdened them before reaching the plateau are the same flaws that undermine them later.

Gord Stellick, the Maple Leafs' assistant general manager when Vaive was captain and now the club's radio color commentator, often watched Rick Vaive and just as often found himself shaking his head. Vaive, it seemed to Stellick, had it all. He had parlayed a Grade 11 education, good skills and fierce determination into the captaincy of one of the best-known teams in the world. He had a wry and beautiful wife with whom he could share his life, and he was a hockey star in a lucrative hockey market. Barring some catastrophic financial decisions, Vaive would be financially secure by the age of 30.

"So much happened quickly. He was making good money, captain of the Maple Leafs, getting married," said Stellick, "but he could just never be happy. He'd think, 'Maybe I can make more money and be happy.' Well, he made more money and he still wasn't happy. All the material things were coming together but he couldn't fully enjoy it."

When the Leafs were losing, and they never finished within shouting distance of .500 during his tenure, Vaive was a picture of sullen anger. He smashed his stick against the net or boards and shouted at himself to do better. Photographs show a player consumed by stress, facial muscles contorted, lips pursed, eyes narrowed. At one practice, he cursed the assistant coach, Dan Maloney, and bolted from the ice. Unlike previous captains who had surrounded themselves with team men, Vaive's closest friends, Bill Derlago and Anderson, were underachievers and poor team players. Except for Joyce, no one could ease the pain.

But Rick Vaive wouldn't trade his Toronto years for the world and he is wise in that. Nothing is quite so instructive as great difficulty, provided, of course, that it is viewed in retrospect. Certainly, Vaive's captaincy was largely undistinguished.

"I look back at it now," Vaive said, "and I realize that I didn't know how to be a captain. I was too young. I don't think I was a total screwup, I mean I think I did some things right and I think I did some things wrong."

It's too simple to say that Rick Vaive should never have been captain of the Toronto Maple Leafs. Under the right circumstances, players of his industry and talent would have thrived. The problem was timing.

When he was appointed, Vaive had the least seniority as a Leaf of all previous captains. He was three weeks younger than Ted Kennedy had been when he was named captain at 22, but Kennedy had been a Leaf for five years. Vaive had been in Toronto a little less than two years.

There were other differences between the two. From the day he arrived in Toronto, Kennedy was schooled by one coach, his mentor, Hap Day. During his seven years in Toronto, Vaive played for Floyd Smith, Dick Duff, Punch Imlach, Joe Crozier, Mike Nykoluk, Dan Maloney and John Brophy.

Because Vaive succeeded Sittler, he was the first person to try to lead the Leafs out of the morass that engulfed the franchise. While Sittler had lieutenants—Tiger Williams, Lanny McDonald and Ron Ellis—to help him, Vaive had no one.

By any statistic, Vaive was an outstanding Maple Leaf, one of the best ever. He scored 441 NHL goals, 299 with the Leafs. He is the only Toronto player ever to record three 50-goal seasons. Vaive, a right-winger, scored more goals than Hall of Fame right-wingers Yvan Cournoyer, Rod Gilbert, Bernie Geoffrion and Andy Bathgate.

"He couldn't have done much more," said Bill Watters, then Vaive's agent and now the Leafs' assistant general manager. "The problem was, the Maple Leafs weren't quite as prominent as they are now. He drew the short straw."

Richard Claude Vaive was born on Ottawa in May 14, 1959, to Mary and Claude Vaive. He learned to skate when he was four years old and his dad helped a neighbor flood a rink at the back of a row of townhouses. Claude, who worked for Dominion Bridge, was transferred to Amherst, Nova Scotia, when Rick was eight. Three years later, his father injured his leg in an industrial accident and the family moved to Charlottetown,

Prince Edward Island, where Claude started a painting business.

Vaive hated school but loved hockey. He met Joyce in Grade 10 and the two began dating. Joyce was an excellent athlete and a member of the Canadian junior basketball team. She is a forthright, down-to-earth woman who still gets ribbed about winning the Miss Congeniality Award at the 1980 Miss Canada Pageant.

Vaive started his major junior career with the Sherbrooke Beavers of the Quebec Major Junior Hockey League where he made $19 a week. He was the QMJHL rookie of the year and the Beavers won the league championship, the only title of Rick Vaive's career. Vaive scored 51 goals his first season and followed up with a 76-goal season the next.

When the WHA's Birmingham Bulls changed hockey's rules by signing 18-year-olds, Vaive was one of the club's prime catches. He earned $50,000 in the 1978–79 season playing for John Bassett's Baby Bulls along with four other underage juniors, including Michel Goulet and future Leafs' captain Rob Ramage. Vaive scored 26 goals in his first year as a pro and was involved in plenty of fights, racking up 248 penalty minutes. When the WHA folded at the end of the season, four teams, Edmonton, New England, Winnipeg and Quebec, transferred to the NHL. Vaive went into the NHL draft and was chosen by Vancouver behind only Ramage, Perry Turnbull and two other eventual Maple Leafs, Mike Foligno and Mike Gartner.

But the Canucks quickly soured on Vaive. Although he scored 13 goals in 47 games, in February, 1980, he was sent to Toronto together with Bill Derlago for Tiger Williams and Jerry Butler.

Vaive was by no means ready to be a pro. He wasn't mature enough, he wasn't fit and the Canucks were wary of his drinking.

"He reported to camp in atrocious shape," said Harry Neale, then the Canucks' coach. "We were worried he wasn't going to get around the bend with reference to him being a complete professional."

Drinking, especially with a veteran team, was part of a pro's life. Vaive wanted to fit in, but he ended up only hurting his career.

The Canucks were equally unhappy with Derlago who showed an early habit of using only a fraction of his abundant talent, a habit he never shook. When the chance came to land two less talented but more dedicated players, Williams and Butler, the club jumped at the chance. Originally the deal was Williams and Butler for Derlago and utility forward Jere Gillis but when Maple Leafs' general manager Punch Imlach insisted on Vaive, the Canucks agreed.

"It wasn't so much that we wanted to get rid of those two players," Neale said, "but Butler and Williams gave us toughness and that was something that we really needed. It was the classic deal that was good for one team's present and the other team's future. Vaive and Derlago played well for the Leafs for a lot of years but Williams helped get us into the finals in 1982."

Vaive thought the deal was too good to be true. He was out of Neale's doghouse and the pressure of being a first-round choice was mostly removed while his ice time was increased. He scored nine more goals in Toronto, including two in his first game, to finish with 22 for his rookie season, and the following season scored 33. He had arrived.

Vaive's success depended on his shot. He was gifted with a terrific shot and he worked tirelessly to hone a hair-trigger release. His stick, which he named Big Bertha, weighed 1.5 pounds, about a third more than the average. The extra weight made his shot heavy as well as fast. Although many of his goals came from bullets delivered from the right, Vaive was willing to plant himself in the slot or crease and absorb boatloads of punishment for a shot on goal.

"I just can't see myself considered with the goal scoring abilities of players like Mike Bossy and Wayne Gretzky," Vaive once told a writer. "Watch how they score their goals. They come in on the net, make fancy moves and pick corners. I just blast away."

Vaive blasted in all directions. He racked up 229 penalty minutes in his first full season and wrestled with his temper, as well as his opponents, whenever he was on the ice. Leafs' fans recognized Vaive's promise and he quickly became a popular player. His obvious effort easily overshadowed a weakness for poorly timed retaliatory penalties and too-long shifts.

Vaive took over as interim captain when Sittler left the team in January, 1982. While the decision to give him the letter would prove poor, the Leafs had little choice. Wilf Paiement, the team's top scorer, had come over in the Lanny McDonald deal and spent only one full season in Toronto before he was dealt to Quebec. Ian Turnbull was too independent, Dan Maloney too old. Derlago and Anderson had no leadership ability. That left only Vaive, the team's brightest young star, and the player who seemed the natural choice, Borje Salming.

But Salming wanted no part of being captain. The veteran defenseman had seen the toll the job had taken on Sittler, and with Ballard in good health nothing was likely to change. Even if he had wanted the job, Salming's relations with referees were uniformly poor and he would have been hard-pressed to gain their ear.

Unlike Salming, Vaive wanted the job, although his wishes hardly mattered to Ballard. Vaive recalls having little choice when Ballard told him in September, 1982, the C would stay.

"I mean, what could I do? There was no discussion. The

owner of one of the most famous franchises in pro sports says, 'You're my captain.' It wasn't a request."

The Leafs knew Vaive was young, both in years and in maturity, but felt that if they kept on stroking him, he would respond. They were partially right. Vaive always played better for coaches who coddled him. But no amount of praise could age him five years.

"I can't tell you how important Rick is in what we're trying to do," Leafs' coach Mike Nykoluk told reporters. "It's imperative this club, with all its kids, has strong internal leadership. Rick, as the guy with the C, will be expected to provide that. We can't succeed without it."

Stellick remembers thinking differently.

"Even though Ricky Vaive didn't ask to be captain, he was anxious to be captain when Darryl left," Stellick said. "That was the killer because he was never a leader. To add to his unhappiness, the captain brought him no happiness at all. And even as a captain, he would go out and do everything right but he just couldn't get the acceptance of a true captain and that just added to his frustration."

Vaive had inherited a team impossible to lead. Salming, the only other player who could have helped, did nothing to back him up.

"Borje was a private guy and I respected that but I could have used the help," Vaive said. "If I said, 'Some guys aren't pulling their weight,' it would have been great to have him say, 'Listen to him, he's our captain, he's right.' But that never happened."

Vaive tried to adopt a persona for which he had no blueprint—the gutsy captain.

"He's always been an easygoing guy and I think the captaincy took that away from him," said Joyce Vaive. "You're not supposed to be easygoing, you're supposed to be leading by example all the time. How do you lead when you're 22, 23, 24, just making some good money, becoming a superstar, and you've got a guy like Borje Salming in the corner of the room? Ian Turnbull was still there and the team was in a shambles because of the Lanny trade the year before."

Vaive threw himself into public relations. Regardless of how the team fared, he answered media questions. He was extraordinarily active in the team's charities. As an honorary chairman for United Appeal, he visited schools and helped raise $80,000 for the charity. He often conscripted teammates for trips to the Hospital for Sick Children.

While the captaincy would eventually become a millstone, it did not immediately pull Vaive under. Vaive had his best three NHL seasons as captain. In March, 1982, he became the first Maple Leaf to break the 50-goal barrier when Derlago stickhandled past two St. Louis Blues and fed Vaive who ripped the puck past Mike Liut. His total that year of 54 goals is still the best in club history.

Vaive scored 51 in 1982–83. The fiftieth again came from Derlago who won a draw from Dwight Foster in the Detroit zone and dropped the puck to Vaive. Vaive proceeded to blast a slapshot past Gilles Gilbert. In 1983–84, he hit for 52, beating Gilles Meloche of the Minnesota North Stars for number 50.

During this run of 50-goal seasons, only Wayne Gretzky and Mike Bossy scored more goals although Vaive never finished among the league's top ten point-getters. But these individual triumphs were tempered by the Leafs' poor play. The Leafs missed the playoffs twice and were ousted in the first round of the playoffs in the other year.

While Vaive continued to score, the frustration of constantly losing was wearing him down.

"It's pretty obvious we can't win with only eight or nine guys giving 100 percent," Vaive told the *Toronto Star* in January, 1983. "It looks like we have some guys who don't like the heavy going. If you gotta take a hit to get the job done, then take it. You can't back down."

In 1985, he berated teammates for dropping their practice jerseys on the floor after a workout. "It's laziness. It starts in here and it carries out on the ice," he shouted at them. "Do you think trainers are maids to pick up after you?"

Like Sittler, Vaive was critical of the way the Leafs discarded veterans whose value had diminished. He also had the inevitable run-ins with Harold Ballard. After Vaive notched his third straight 50-goal season, Ballard called him a journeyman.

"If he played on the old Montreal Canadiens or Leaf clubs, he would have been just a mediocre player. He stands out on this team only because of the caliber of players around him," Ballard told the media.

"I just think Rick was extremely frustrated with the fact that his personal goals were wonderful but deep down he wanted to win the Stanley Cup," said Joyce Vaive.

Vaive's problems were exacerbated when the Leafs fired Nykoluk, a gentle man, and brought in Dan Maloney. Maloney and Vaive had blown hot and cold when Maloney was an assistant coach, and the two were incompatible. As a player, Maloney had a fraction of Vaive's talent but thrived as a tough-minded fighter. He saw Vaive as mentally soft and tried to harden him by chiding him for the inconsistencies in his leadership. When Vaive begged off a training camp run because of a sore back but greeted teammates at the finish line with a coffee and a cigarette, Maloney was incensed.

Vaive, meanwhile, saw Maloney as just another in a growing list of critics. He was too confused and isolated to know who his friends were.

"Some mornings I'd wake up and wish I wouldn't have to go to work," Vaive said. "It was so depressing. I was worried that, as a captain, I was supposed to be a leader and I didn't contribute." The *Toronto Star*'s Jim Proudfoot wrote that Vaive passed up good scoring chances to appear unselfish. To demonstrate his commitment to winning, Vaive structured his 1984 contract to emphasize team rather than individual bonuses.

For whatever reason, Vaive didn't play well in 1984–85. His ice time was reduced and his scoring slumped to 35 goals. Maloney benched him for one entire game. Fittingly, it was the Leafs' 46th loss, a club record.

The 1985–86 season was much the same. Vaive's unhappiness was growing but at least the Leafs, under Maloney, were showing signs of improvement. Then the roof caved in for Vaive.

On February 21, Vaive and the Leafs were in Minneapolis. The Leafs had played the Minnesota North Stars the night before and were scheduled to practice the next morning before they flew. The Quebec Nordiques, John Anderson's current team, were also in town to play the Stars, so the two old friends got together after the Minnesota–Toronto game.

The next morning, Vaive didn't answer the bell. At first Maloney told the media that Vaive was ill with the flu but later that same day, Ballard and Gerry McNamara, the general manager, decided to take his captaincy away. On February 22, 1986, the title Vaive had held for almost five years was stripped from him.

"Rick missed practice this morning and as a result we've removed the C from his sweater," a stone-faced McNamara told the media. "He will no longer be captain. I say this with great regret, but I don't think we had any other recourse. It was a painful decision."

In fact, the Leafs had a very real choice. Vaive's breach was certainly serious, especially for the club's captain, but only a fraction of the stupidities committed by players on the road go reported in the media. There was ample precedence for reprimanding but not demoting Vaive.

"Basically, I screwed up. I went out with an old buddy, got into the sauce a little too much and slept in," Vaive said from Charleston. "I've known a lot of guys who were gone for days and the coach went to bat for him. He also said, 'This isn't going to happen again. Here's the story, now stick to it'."

In retrospect, the Leafs' hypocrisy was astonishing. Ballard was a foul-mouthed tyrant, a convicted criminal whose public pronouncements on women and minorities would have been laughable if they were not so offensive. Any drive toward excellence had long since been blunted by the team's pathetic scouting and training budgets. McNamara was waging a bitter, paranoid war with members of the Toronto media. When the *Globe and Mail* hockey writer displeased Ballard, the paper was forced to buy a seat to cover the remaining season. The club's proud history had long since been obscured by Ballard's buffoonery.

Yet when Rick Vaive had too many beers one night and overslept, he was judged to be morally deficient.

The move raised eyebrows around the league.

"What happened last Saturday would make a lot of people suspicious," an unnamed NHL GM told the *Toronto Star*'s Jim Proudfoot. "The story was the Leafs took away the captaincy because Vaive slept in and missed a practice. Well, that's pretty bad but my reaction is there's got to be more to it than that."

There was. The Maple Leafs recognized their mistake in appointing Vaive captain. But given the choice between accepting some of the responsibility or saving face, they opted to trash Vaive.

"He just wasn't the right temperament for a captain. In a nutshell, he just wasn't a leader," Ballard told the *Globe and Mail*. "I don't think he was good material for a captain and I selected him years ago."

The captaincy seemed cursed. Until 1982, only one Leafs' captain, Bob Davidson, had failed to make an all-star team. By Vaive's demotion, the captaincy had become a burden.

"Just as Groucho Marx said he wouldn't want to be a member of any club that would have him as a member, the Leafs should avoid giving their captaincy to anyone who would accept it willingly," Frank Orr wrote in the *Hockey News*. "After what happened to the last three men who held the post (Keon, Sittler and now Vaive), such an act would indicate the lack of a well-occupied upper story."

Vaive was impressive during the media inquisition that followed. He didn't duck interviews, he admitted his mistake and he said he accepted the consequences, never suggesting how ludicrously out of proportion the punishment was to the crime.

"That was the way the organization was run," Bill Watters remembered. "I mean, they embarrassed themselves by doing it. Something like that could very easily have been said, 'Hey, let's not let it happen again.'"

Vaive has long since come to terms with the incident. "I can't do anything about it now. I can't turn the clock back. There's no sense in destroying your life and killing yourself over something you can't change. But that's not to say that even today it doesn't creep back into your mind and you say, 'Oh, damn, I did screw up. What might have happened had I not done that? How would things have turned out? Where would I be today if that hadn't happened?'"

The loss of the captaincy turbocharged trade rumors coming from the Gardens but in fact Vaive outlasted Maloney.

The Maple Leafs improved their point total by nine to 57 and made the playoffs in 1985–86 but when Maloney asked for a contract extension, Ballard offered a meager one-year deal for $75,000. Maloney quit and was barely out the door when the Winnipeg Jets signed him to coach. Even though the two had quarreled, Vaive thought Maloney was a good coach and backed him publicly.

"I've heard that Dan wasn't happy with the offer and I don't blame him," Vaive told reporters. "I think Dan's resignation is really bad for the hockey club at this point in time. We were just starting to come together as a team and then this happens."

Vaive had been supplanted both as captain and as the team's star. Wendel Clark arrived in 1985 and posted a sensational 34-goal rookie season. As Vaive had done a half a dozen years earlier, Clark stirred hopes that a good team might be just around the corner. Vaive was no longer a 50-goal scorer. In fact, his failings were a constant reminder of the club's mismanagement and fans began to boo him.

The difficulty of his situation was clearly shown one night in 1986 when the Leafs beat the New York Rangers 7–3. Clark scored three times and was cheered wildly as the game's first star. Vaive, the third star, was heavily booed. The young captain experiment had soured so badly with Vaive that management did not risk bestowing the letter on another young player. Instead, the Leafs went without a captain from 1986 to 1989.

John Brophy took over the Leafs in 1986–87 and Vaive scored 32 times, but it was the first season in five he did not lead the team in goals. As Clark's star ascended, Vaive's was clearly falling.

A rib injury sidelined Vaive in the second round of the playoffs as the Leafs lost in seven games to Detroit. Vaive wept when he couldn't play. Ironically, at the end of his Toronto career he was receiving much of the respect he had worked so hard for earlier. Even Vaive's detractors admitted he had handled himself well after losing the captaincy, and his supporters, believing his trade was imminent, rallied around him.

"To me, he can't be replaced," an emotional Brad Smith

told writers after the loss to Detroit. "He's my captain, my leader out there. He is just a great player. I can't carry his skates to the rink."

Vaive would not play another game for the Leafs. He and the club agreed to terms on a one-year, $300,000 contract for the next season but he wasn't offered a raise on a long-term deal. On September 3, 1987, Vaive, along with Bob McGill and Steve Thomas, was traded to Chicago for Al Secord and Ed Olczyk.

Thomas had generated the deal by complaining about the Leafs' obvious lack of scouting personnel and by asking for a raise from $80,000 to $270,000. But for Vaive, the end was merciful. It ended years of speculation and allowed the Leafs' management to bury a mistake.

"There was always something about Rick," said Bill Watters. "They couldn't very well demote him—all he did was score 50 goals per year. But I think they thought by trading Rick, it would make them a better team. In retrospect, they traded Rick Vaive for Al Secord, one of the worst trades in the history of the team."

Because Vaive's old number 22 was held by former teammate Gary Nylund in Chicago, Vaive wore 44. Playing for Bob Murdoch, a positive, encouraging coach in the mold of Mike Nykoluk, Vaive responded with a 43-goal year, but whatever good luck he had walked into didn't last.

The Hawks fired Murdoch in the off-season and replaced him with Mike Keenan, Vaive's worst nightmare. Keenan was abrasive with players and unforgiving of those who didn't meet his standards.

Vaive, a mostly one-dimensional player whose offensive production would not improve, was at the top of that list. He was benched for the first half of the season but nonetheless studied Keenan's tactics.

"Mike Keenan was one of the best coaches I ever played for," Vaive says now. "His teams are always prepared. His practices are the best I've ever seen. But he can be very cutting and I've seen that firsthand."

Knowing that the clock was running out on his career, Vaive requested a trade. The Blackhawks complied and sent him to Buffalo for Adam Creighton, a tall center who had underachieved with the Sabres and who would thrive under Keenan.

The pounding he had absorbed throughout his career began to affect Vaive's productivity. He wore a neck brace to protect himself from cross-checks but, while he managed 31, 29 and 25 goals over the next three seasons, his stock was falling quickly. At 32, in 1992, Vaive was let go by the Sabres and nobody else wanted him. Determined to play and perhaps to reestablish some value in time for a shot with Ottawa or Tampa Bay in the expansion draft, Vaive asked to be sent down to the Sabres' affiliate in the American Hockey League, the Rochester Americans.

In Rochester, Vaive found much more playing time and an immediate role as an elder statesman. He loved it.

"I could sense the respect of the younger players and I could tell they were listening to me when I'd tell them something," Vaive said. When the Senators turned down his offer to play for the NHL minimum, Vaive took a job as a playing assistant with the AHL's Hamilton Canucks. Being a quasi-player, quasi-coach was uncomfortable but it nonetheless confirmed to Vaive that he wanted to coach.

"What really got me going was when I was an assistant in Hamilton. Being in training camp, I sat around with the scouts and the general managers and I found that very, very interesting. I had no idea what went on behind the scenes. Right then and there, I said I want to be part of it."

This time, Vaive was determined to start from the bottom. He called the East Coast Hockey League in the summer of 1993 and asked to be put in touch with any franchise owner with a coaching vacancy. A few weeks later, he was in South Carolina.

The ECHL operates with a weekly salary cap of $6,000 a week, or about $350 a week per player with an apartment provided. The top players make only about $10,000 a season. The league is staffed by career minor leaguers—skill players who are too small, tough players who can't skate, goalies whose game has gone south.

It's here that Rick Vaive is putting all the mistakes he made, and those made by others regarding Vaive, to work.

"I don't always do the right things, I don't always make the right decisions, but I try to be fair with the guys," Vaive said. "If they're not playing, I tell them why. I don't ever want a player I coached to walk away and say, 'Goddamn guy lied to me,' or 'He wasn't fair to me.' I want everyone to have a chance."

This time, Vaive is making his own timetable. He wants to apprentice in the low minors before thinking about an American or International Hockey League job.

"I'm not ready and I don't want to make the same mistake again. Over the last years, I'd say I've improved 50 percent as coach, and my goal is to keep improving and get to the next level."

The holy grail of the NHL is behind him. Rick Vaive has finally found what he's been looking for.

"My life is fabulous," said Vaive. "I mean I'm the luckiest guy I know. I love my job. I have a great wife and two great boys. I won't kid you and say I don't miss scoring a goal and having 15,000 people cheering. I miss it a lot—but I'm happy."

CHAPTER 8

WENDEL CLARK

CAPTAIN, 1991–94

July 1, 1994

As Wendel Clark wiped away a tear, the makeshift podium was covered by a firestorm of flashes. For photographers, reporters and eyewitnesses jammed into Don Cherry's Mississauga restaurant on Canada Day, 1994, it was a sight never before imagined, let alone witnessed and preserved on film.

No one in the room thought Wendel Clark couldn't be traded. Coming off a 46-goal season and back-to-back campaigns of more than 60 games played, the Maple Leafs' captain had made himself more marketable than he had been in a decade.

The media had traded Clark on countless occasions but this time it was for real. Wendel Clark had been dealt to the Quebec Nordiques. While the idea of Clark playing anywhere but in Toronto seemed incongruous, the acquisition of Mats Sundin, eased the club's most pressing long-term problem, a lack of young talent at center.

What had begun as a photo opportunity, a chance for Clark to publicly comment on his trade, became something much more in the moments when his voice wavered and he wiped a tear from his eye. He showed, for an instant, what was inside. "Real men," said the *Toronto Sun*, "do cry."

Mary Ormsby's lead in the *Toronto Star* the next day read simply, "Wendel Clark cried."

"When I'm around friends I don't get that emotional," Clark said in what was, even for him, a monumental understatement. "This is probably the worst I've been in nine years."

Sorrow, let alone a tear, was something Wendel Clark had never publicly allowed himself. When they saw the clip on the national news in Kelvington, Saskatchewan, Les and Alma Clark were stunned.

"I have never seen Wendel like that, not in public, not ever," said his father. The last time Alma had seen her son cry was when Les and Wendel quarreled over where Wendel would play junior hockey. Wendel wanted to play in Saskatoon and eventually did. Les was set on Regina or Prince Albert.

The Clarks have often cried for their son. "I cried many a time when he was playing the game or scoring a goal," said Les. Alma remembers being devastated at the sight of her son in his third NHL season, at home in Kelvington because of an ailing back, in too much pain to sit or stand for five minutes at a time.

But Wendel never cried. Not when he was two years old and Les took him to the center of the ice of the Kelvington Arena and left him either to skate or crawl back to the boards before being carried back to center again.

Not when he left home for good at 15 to play hockey in Regina. Not when he missed more than 100 games with the Leafs because of his terribly injured back, or when his play and often his courage were attacked on the street, in print and on air.

Through his decade in Toronto, Clark observed one rule: Never complain, never explain. He arrived in Toronto in 1985 as the league's overall first draft choice. He mastered a new position when the Leafs switched him from defense to left wing to become one of the league's most highly regarded rookies. He fought all comers and supplied a glimmer of hope in a dark chapter in the club's history.

He lost his career to injury and then regained it by overhauling his body as well as his instinct always to play and always to punish. He survived years of rumors, both about possible trades and about his sex life. He was Toronto's most charismatic player since Darryl Sittler, and he captained the Leafs for three seasons under the scrutiny of excitable media.

Through it all, Wendel Clark did everything he could to make himself immune to public displays of emotion. But for that final press conference, he would have pulled it off.

Said his agent and friend, Don Meehan, who wept at Clark's side, "I was so very proud of him."

Although Clark speaks to the media whenever asked, his remarks are the usual collection of clichés in which athletes and journalists trade. The man who wears a belt buckle with the words "Just a Farmer" provides few details or analysis about his injuries, his feelings or anything else. In his first years in Toronto, his lack of introspection was seen as a lack of intelligence. Admirers later attributed it to western Canadian stoicism.

Clark was awkward around people when he first came into the league. "I'm still that way today," Clark said over breakfast in the coffee shop of a Buffalo hotel. "If I don't know someone, I don't speak. If I'm more open now, it's because I've been in the league ten years and know more people."

As a young player, he knew little of the world outside his sport but he is an intelligent man. Despite a rigorous hockey schedule, Clark was an A student in high school and at Notre Dame College; he particularly excelled in algebra. His instincts with people, though cautious, are unfailingly accurate and his personal code is unyieldingly honorable. He refused, for example, to use his trade to Quebec to leverage a raise from the Nordiques, although grumbling about the cultural and linguistic adjustments necessary to live in Quebec City has become an accepted path to secure a heftier paycheque.

"If another player feels comfortable with it, that's fine," Clark said. "But I can walk anywhere in the league and not feel uncomfortable looking anyone in the face and saying I did it the way I wanted."

That comment is as close as Wendel Clark comes to explaining himself. During a decade in Toronto, he supplied the play but let others provide the commentary. His silence complemented his style.

"If you can't understand what Wendel Clark is all about by the way he plays and what he contributes, your expectations are unreasonable," argues Don Meehan. "All you have to do is talk to someone in the dressing room. He doesn't have to explain himself and you shouldn't expect it."

It's natural to judge a player's personality by what we see on the ice. Players who avoid the corners are believed to be cowards and morally deficient. Players like Clark who fight the biggest and strongest competitors are praised for their courage. When they stop, because of injury or age or strategy, their virtues also seem to fade.

It isn't that simple, of course. We are both more and less than the sum total of our work. Dave Keon's on-ice image of a polished star never jibed with his prickly off-ice personality. Hockey thugs are often introspective; John Kordic's dissatisfaction with his role as goon led to his collapse. Clark gave fans (and journalists) only his play by which to judge him but the unbridled passion he brought to the ice in his first two seasons was misleading. He is above all a measured man.

In his rookie season, Clark threw up before every game. When he realized this was leaving him with little energy, Clark stopped. Just that easily. Logic, as it always has with Clark, won out over emotion. In the farm boy from Saskatchewan, Toronto reporters encountered a stolid figure who refused to acknowledge the turmoil around him.

"There's always times you can be the maddest person in the world about something that happened that day," Clark said at breakfast, "but if you blow up over it, it may have repercussions for the entire year. Whereas, if you can work your way through that one incident, it might be smooth sailing for the rest of the year."

Whenever reporters asked about a trade rumor, Clark would shrug and say it was something over which he had no control. When Harold Ballard told the media that Clark was a malingerer because he wouldn't play, Clark said he was entitled to his opinion. In a business fueled by ego, Clark never lashed out, never protested, never claimed greatness.

"You play with your brain more than you play with your ego," Clark said after devouring a bowl of porridge. "You play hard all the time but, when you play with your brain, you do what's right for the long term. When you play with your ego, you do what's right for now."

His brain, sometimes at cross purposes with his brawn, has kept Clark in the NHL. When it seemed a severe back injury would end his career, he and Meehan took over his medical care, interviewed scores of specialists and searched the globe until they found treatments that would help Clark become healthy. He now hands out punishment on the ice judiciously, enough to scotch any rumors he has gone soft, not too much to risk new injury unnecessarily. He can recognize within moments of waking up what his body will allow him to do that day. During a pregame warm-up, Clark mentally inventories his capabilities, the better to maximize them during a game.

"What Wendel has a lot of," said Nordiques' coach Marc

Crawford and a former Leafs' assistant coach, "is common sense. When you have a common sense approach to your life and your game, it makes you a good player."

"He has a way, or a habit, of making things less complicated," said Meehan. "He has a demeanor that is readily accepted by everybody. It strikes you as a straight common sense approach but with all the sincerity and conviction that anyone can have."

At breakfast Clark shook his head when asked if he was an intelligent man.

"No," he smiled. "Simple."

"Simple good or simple bad?"

"Just simple. The simpler I can keep things, the easier it is to make decisions. That way, it's easier for me to understand what I should do."

The real answer is simple good.

"The thing I've always liked about Wendel," said Gord Stellick, "is that he never forgot who he was or where he was from. A lot of players do. Wendel never did."

Not forgetting where he was from and who he was made Clark a hero in Toronto and persuaded the Nordiques to trade a franchise player to acquire him.

"There isn't a general manager in the league who wouldn't want him on his team," said Clark's cousin, Rangers' winger Joey Kocur. "And there isn't a player in the league who wouldn't want him as a teammate."

Les Clark helped build Kelvington's indoor arena in 1978 and then he ran it for 10 years. It seemed natural. His father, Robert Clark, helped to build the town's first indoor skating rink in 1947.

When he played his first NHL game in 1985, Wendel Clark

completed a journey his father had begun. Les Clark was born in Kelvington but left home at 15 to play junior hockey in Humboldt, Moose Jaw, Saskatoon and Prince Albert. After five years of junior, he turned pro and labored for four years in minor league towns such as Troy, Ohio, and Charlotte, North Carolina. "I wasn't good enough to play. That's why I went from place to place," he says matter-of-factly.

A broken leg ended a sometimes controversial but largely undistinguished career. In junior, Clark was suspended for a year for charging a goal judge. The incident would have been less spectacular if the netting surrounding the official had not been improperly installed. The rigging crashed down but league officials refused any leniency to Les Clark based on faulty equipment.

When he returned to Kelvington, Clark met Alma Pinder, an elementary school teacher, at a dance. The two married two years later and began working the Clark family's 500-acre ranch. They had three sons, Donn, Wendel and Kerry. Alma named all three boys from a book of baby names.

The boys were encouraged to play hockey from the beginning. Les's day was spent doing chores and in the family's early years Alma kept her teaching job. All babysitters were issued strict instructions that Donn was to spend 15 minutes in the morning and 15 minutes at night in skates on the linoleum floor in the kitchen. Donn's hockey career was cut short by a badly broken leg suffered in junior hockey. He is now the head coach of the Western League's Prince Albert Raiders. Kerry is a minor leaguer in the Washington Capitals' system.

Wendel was the smallest child. When he was four, he shared his clothes with his two-and-a-half-year-old brother. An outdoor rink was only a short walk away and a hockey-playing big brother was the only motivation Wendel and Kerry needed.

Les Clark values intimidation in hockey. When he noticed

that Kerry was timid in the corners, he knocked him down in the kitchen with a shoulder check. When Kerry got up, Les knocked him down again.

"Did that hurt?" Les asked his son.

"No," said Kerry.

"Then why are you afraid to go into the corner? Go in fast—it's not going to hurt you."

Raising livestock left little leisure time but the Clark boys filled every available moment with sports. Wendel played softball in the summer and hockey in the winter. His coaches saw far more of Wendel's play than his father did. When he watched them, Les found himself shouting for his boys to try harder. When the frustration welled up inside him, he would leave the rink.

Wendel has inherited Les's perfectionism. "Les always wanted more," said Alma Clark. "I remember, he was coaching [former Los Angeles Kings' coach] Barry Melrose, and he'd be on the side of the boards yelling, 'Faster, Barry. Faster, Barry.' But that was as fast as Barry could go. That's what Les believed, as high as you go, you still strive to be better."

When Wendel showed himself clearly better than the other 12-year-old bantams, Les decided that rather than playing in the next age group, Wendel should play bantam in Yorkton, 93 miles away.

"I didn't want him to go up in age, I wanted him to stay in his own age level and have better quality," Les Clark said. "When you get a boy who's 14 years old going against another who's 17 in midget, the young one can lose his confidence."

By now, Les knew he was dealing with a prodigy, and it was just as clear to others. St. Louis Blues' star Bernie Federko remembered Wendel from his Saskatoon hockey school.

"This kid was 11 years old, he worked hard, had a lot of fun, was everyone's friend and didn't seem to mind a little rough stuff," Federko said after Clark turned pro. "You just sort of knew from day one that he would amount to something in hockey."

Alma had left her teaching job and it fell to her to drive Wendel to Yorkton for games and practices. It was a three-and-a-half hour round trip made as often as five times a week. One year, with both Wendel and Kerry in junior, the family put 65,000 kilometers on their car. Alma would doze in the car during the practice, the better to fight sleep on the way home. Wendel would do his homework on the way up, often with his mother as a tutor, and sleep on the way home.

Regardless of how late the boys returned to the farm, they were expected to be up for the school bus the next morning. While he waited for the bus, Wendel would often practice his shot on a piece of slippery wood veneer.

"Even if they got home at 4:30 in the morning or five, they had to get up for school the next day," said Les. "Here are boys out all night, sometimes travelling 500 miles, and they were at school the next morning. There were some boys who had to travel half a mile and couldn't make it to school."

"We wondered if we were doing the right thing, whether it was too much for him to be up that late," said Alma. "And then we'd see his friends still up roaming the street at midnight or 1 a.m. Then we knew it wasn't too late for him."

The two seasons in Yorkton convinced Les and Wendel that he was ready for elite play. Notre Dame College in Wilcox, Saskatchewan, a 400-person private high school, was the natural choice.

Not everyone in the family agreed that Wendel was old enough at 15 to attend school so far from home.

"My mom and dad, they didn't want him to go but I said he has to," Les said. "If he's going to get better in hockey, he has to have competition."

"Basically, it [the school] was well known for great hockey," said Wendel. "The hockey was better than you could get playing in small towns. Otherwise you would have to go to the city to play. This way, I was put in Notre Dame boarding school; I knew I was going to go to school and play hockey."

Les and Alma knew that the values they had worked to instill were as entrenched as they would ever be. Their son made an immediate impact at Notre Dame.

"As a defenseman, he was so smooth on his skates," said Hounds' coach Barry MacKenzie. "People might think that they were by him and they would be the victim of a bonecrusher check. He loved to hit, he had a real knack. To him it was always part of the game and something that came easy."

By his second season at Notre Dame, Clark was heading toward a pro career. But even when Wendel moved to Saskatoon to play for the Western Hockey League Blades, a major junior team, Les and Alma's rules still applied. Clark packed high school and study sessions into and around road trips.

"Wendel's first year of junior, with all the road trips, he missed five days of high school," said Les. "I had a deal with our boys. If they missed school, they were done. I paid them so much a month and I had them under the gun. If they crossed me, they didn't have to worry about their coach or anybody else. If they crossed me they were in trouble."

"With the traveling and stuff, I always told him, if I ever once have to call you at home in the morning or you don't get your work done, that's it for hockey," Alma said. "Just one time."

His parents remain the most important people in Clark's life. His work ethic comes from both parents, the ruggedness through Les, the sense of reason from his mother. "Alma was the mediator in the family," recalls Joey Kocur. "Les had a temper but Alma smoothed the waters wherever she went."

"Everything you are comes from your parents," Wendel

said. "You're never bigger than what you do. You play hockey for four years, that's the average, ten years if you're very fortunate, but the same road you go up, you've got to come back down."

In his first season with the Blades as a 17-year-old defenseman, Clark scored 23 goals, recorded 68 points and racked up 225 penalty minutes. He upped those totals to 32 goals, 87 points and 253 minutes in his second season. Clark's rugged style earned him his share of injuries but he proved to be almost impossible to sit down. When he separated his shoulder in his draft year, Clark agreed to sit out one game and then told his coaches to either play him or trade him. His competitiveness and unwillingness to accept injuries raised his stock among scouts but would take a heavy toll later.

"He was the hardest-working guy on the ice so he made it easy for a coach," said Blades' coach Daryl Lubiniecki. "Basically everyone followed his lead."

Clark's first fight in junior was a clear decision over Regina's John Minor. The Pats were goading players into fights and then turtling and this tactic was costing the Blades penalties. Wendel got permission from Lubiniecki to fight, but only if a Regina player had landed the first punch and declared his intentions.

"He didn't know if he could fight," said Lubiniecki. "But he threw his punches all the way from Kelvington. When I asked him about it after, he was just bubbling. He was pretty proud of himself."

Clark fought long bouts with Ken Baumgartner, then the resident tough guy of the Prince Albert Raiders. "I used to say, 'Wendel, why are you fighting Baumgartner? You're our best player,' " Lubiniecki said. "'You don't have to fight him—go fight their top scorer.' And Wendel said, 'Well, their top scorer won't fight'."

Clark got his first taste of international competition at the 1985 World Junior Championships in Helsinki, Finland. On New Year's Day, he scored the game-tying goal against Czechoslovakia to earn Canada the gold medal. In an earlier pivotal win over the Soviet Union, Clark had hit Mikhail Tatarinov with a clean check that separated the Russian's shoulder and turned the game around.

The NHL draft that year was held in Toronto. The event at the Metro Convention Centre would prove a benchmark for the Maple Leafs. In the 1984–85 season, the Leafs had bottomed out with 20 wins and 48 points in 80 games, their lowest total since they earned 47 points in a 48-game schedule in 1938–39. While the club featured the promise of some younger talent— Al Iafrate, Russ Courtnall and Gary Leeman (the latter two former Hounds) were being worked into the lineup—the Leafs were at a definite low point.

Ballard had established himself as the center of the franchise and the Leafs spent little time and money on scouting. The McDonald-Sittler years, the club's only period as a contender since 1967, were now a bitter memory and the performance of Rick Vaive, the club's best player, was deteriorating. The atmosphere was so corrosive that the Leafs went without a regular captain. Craig Redmond, considered one of the top half-dozen prospects that year, wrote the Leafs to tell them he thought playing in Toronto would injure his career and he would not report if drafted. Redmond's comments created a sensation in Toronto and prompted reporters to ask other prospects if they would mind playing for the Maple Leafs.

To Clark, the question was absurd.

"I won't be doing anything like that," Clark told reporters. "Whoever wants me, I'll go."

Clark, then as now, was represented by Don Meehan although Meehan was actually the family's second choice.

Wendel had enjoyed a good rapport with an agent named Norm Kaplan, but he died of a heart attack at the age of 37 during Clark's second year of junior.

Clark was considered the best all-around player in the draft, but the Leafs debated choosing Clark or Michigan State alumnus Craig Simpson, a skillful player whom scouts believed had more offensive potential. Ballard would later tell the media that Clark had been the Leafs' first choice all along but, for Clark, the relief was palpable when he was chosen.

"That was probably the most nervous time in your life. Not knowing when or where you're going to go. I just wanted to play in the NHL. As long as you had a chance to play, that's the whole key when you're 18 years old."

Clark signed a four-year, $630,000 deal. He earned $90,000 in his first year, $110,000 in his second, $130,000 in his third and $150,000 in his fourth. The deal also included a $150,000 signing bonus.

In spite of these newfound riches, Wendel Clark arrived in Toronto looking every inch the 19-year-old farm boy. He wore a cowboy hat, and his pants were too long.

Clark had played only about 20 games at forward for the Blades and Team Canada when he arrived in camp, but Leafs' coach Dan Maloney, desperate for some punch from the left side, used him at left wing. Greg Terrion's 14 goals the season before had been the best for a Leafs' left-winger. Leafs' left-wingers in 1984–85 scored only 47 goals, third worst in the league. Only Pittsburgh and Washington fared worse. The Quebec Nordiques, by comparison, scored 137 goals from this position and the Leafs' Norris Division rivals, the Minnesota North Stars, netted 123.

"I have more experience on defense but I'll play wherever they think I can help them," Clark said to reporters when asked about the position change. "My goal is to make the team."

Clark immediately established himself physically. He fought four times in exhibition games and battled in scrimmages. When he made the team, he took on the league's toughest—John Kordic, Rick Tocchet and Behn Wilson.

By February, Clark had fought Terry Johnson, Mark Johnson and Dwight Schofield of the St. Louis Blues, Kelly Miller of the New York Rangers, Edmonton's Marty McSorley, Bob Rouse of the Minnesota North Stars, Troy Loney of the Pittsburgh Penguins, Neil Sheehy of Calgary and Detroit Red Wings John Barrett, Randy Ladouceur and Reed Larson.

"I always fought," Clark shrugged. "Two years of junior I fought 285 and 240 minutes. Pro, I had 200 minutes every year. It was the way I played. I never tried to establish anything other than the fact that I looked after myself and played the way I thought I had to."

Clark even found time to settle an old family score. Garth Butcher and Donn Clark had clashed often when Butcher played for the Regina Pats and Donn for the Blades. On his first shift against St. Louis, Wendel flattened Butcher and the two fought later in the game.

Fiery St. Louis Blues' captain Brian Sutter became one of Clark's earliest admirers. "When a situation that happens on the ice calls for a scrap, Clark gets to it, does it and then skates to the penalty box with no baloney," said Sutter. "There are a lot of guys in this league who talk one hell of a good fight from the bench or after the linesman gets there. Not Clark."

Clark was equally damaging with his gloves on. He roamed the ice looking for players with their heads down and knocked one, the Blues' Bruce Bell, out cold.

Maloney, who used Clark on a line with Russ Courtnall and Gary Leeman, was ecstatic. "I've seen a lot of nights when he's lifted the whole team by getting involved," he said to the *Globe and Mail* after one game. "In the 16 years I've been involved in pro hockey, I've never seen a kid come along like him before."

Clark missed 14 games with a broken foot but that didn't stop King Clancy from calling him the best Leafs' rookie in 50 years. Writers began touting him as a rookie of the year and the Clark for the Calder campaign began in earnest. The Leafs hadn't had a Calder winner since Brit Selby won in 1966 and fans were eager for some long-overdue trophies.

"That was probably the most fun I had in hockey aside from the two playoff runs we had," Clark said. "Playing in the NHL, that's what you want to do your whole life and I was finally doing it."

Campbell Conference coach Glen Sather named Clark to the all-star team and the Leafs' rookie, unaware of the game's tradition of non-contact, raised eyebrows by jolting Mark Howe and Bryan Trottier with stiff checks.

Still, Clark was far from the runaway choice for rookie of the year. His game had enormous holes. He knew little about his position and received little help. While his hits were impressive, he was often out of sync with the play, and his playmaking skills were poor. Two other rookies showed better all-around skills. Gary Suter had stepped into the Calgary Flames' lineup as a significant player and Kjell Dahlin was turning heads with a 32-goal, 71-point rookie season with the Montreal Canadiens.

"Statistics shouldn't be the be-all and end-all when it comes to selecting the best rookie, but on the evidence, Clark comes across as being little more than Reggie Fleming with a better touch around the net," wrote *Globe* sports editor Paul Palango.

Dahlin also questioned whether Clark deserved the award.

"I find it difficult to understand a guy like Wendel Clark winning rookie of the year. He only has 10 assists." Dahlin rated himself, Suter and Mike Ridley ahead of Clark.

The comments were perfect fodder for controversy, but Clark dismissed them out of hand.

"I wasn't there when he made those statements," Clark told reporters. "But I like to look at the better side of it. All the guys he mentioned are good hockey players. Dahlin's certainly a good one. Anybody who gets 65 points is obviously doing a good job."

In the 1986 playoffs, the Leafs swept Chicago in a best-of-five series and battled the Blues to a seventh game before losing the Norris Division final. Clark scored five goals in those ten playoff games including one on an end-to-end rush in game seven against St. Louis. His final regular season total of 34 goals included a hat trick against the New York Rangers and set a club record for rookies. Still, Clark's inadequacies as a playmaker were obvious in his paltry total of 11 assists. While Clark finished second in the rookie of the year balloting with 165 points behind Suter's 230, both *Sporting News* and *The Hockey News* named him their rookie of the year.

It had been a remarkable season and one built largely on desire. Clark was so intense that he threw up before every game. But no one, least of all an average-sized 5'10" 190-pound forward could be expected to keep up the pace.

"He works real hard but he's going to have a hard time maintaining it if he keeps playing like that," said Sather before a midseason game. "If he keeps running into guys who are 210 and 215, he's going to get hurt once in a while. It's a tough style to maintain."

That night Clark had a goal and two assists and clobbered Lee Fogolin, Marty McSorley and Randy Gregg with crunching bodychecks.

Clark delivered much the same results in his sophomore season, scoring 37 goals while playing in all 80 regular season games and 13 playoff games. John Brophy had replaced

Maloney, who quit over a contract problem. Despite Brophy's plan to move Clark back to defense, he played only a few shifts on the blue line when injuries decimated the regulars.

Brophy began to work with Clark on his positioning. Clark began to make fewer big hits but improved, however modestly, his defensive play. He scored four goals in a 5–5 tie against Buffalo in October and the Leafs enjoyed more post-season success, dispatching the Blues in six games to advance against Detroit in the Norris Division final.

The Detroit series was Clark's first brush with bad publicity and began a free-fall in his fortunes.

Clark was enjoying a great playoffs until the Wings began sending out his cousin, Joey Kocur, as a shadow. The move was a master stroke by Detroit coach Jacques Demers. Sportswriters urged Clark to pummel Kocur but he refused. Suddenly, as it would six years later, Clark's willingness to fight became the focal point of a series. "I'll fight you if you don't quit asking me about fighting him," an exasperated Clark told a radio reporter, barely in jest.

Throughout the NHL there are players who will not fight certain other players. Perhaps, like Clark and Kocur, they are related. Often they have been longtime teammates. Regardless, the issue in this series was a sensational red herring. Fighting Kocur was precisely what the Red Wings wanted from Clark. It would remove Clark from the ice with a minuscule sacrifice.

"I wouldn't say we wouldn't fight, but it's the closest thing there was to never fighting," Kocur said. "Wendel was killing us that year and they just had me follow him around the ice, not to play, just to follow him. We played each other clean and it was some of the best times I've ever had in hockey."

The Wings rallied from a 3–1 deficit to win the series in seven games and Clark, who was playing with a sore shoulder, was held at least partially responsible.

By the beginning of Clark's third season, Glen Sather's prophecy was coming true. His body was beginning to break down. His right shoulder was chronically troubled by tendinitis, a condition that was later traced to the shoulder separation suffered as a Blade. Slamming his right shoulder into an opponent caused bruising and inflammation of the tendons surrounding the joint between the arm and the shoulder.

Some doctors believe the shoulder injury Clark suffered in the 1985–86 playoffs was the cause of his back trouble. He reinjured the shoulder in training camp in 1986–87 and began to compensate by relying more heavily on the muscles on the left side of his back. Eventually, doctors theorized, those muscles became much stronger than the ones on his right side and his spine bent.

Clark began the 1987–88 season with back pain so intense it often left his left leg limp. He missed 23 games and then returned to the lineup, scoring eight goals in 17 games. But after uncorking a slapshot in Philadelphia, Clark took himself out of the lineup.

He was beginning the greatest challenge of his career. Clark would not play again for one year and 25 days. Public pressure mounted steadily to get Clark back in the lineup, but while the pain was unbearable, the Maple Leafs' doctors could find no cause, let alone a solution.

Newspaper magnate Ken Thomson recommended an osteopath in London, England. Clark also tried the renowned Mayo Clinic in Minnesota. "The answer was just trying to find someone who could help. London, England, was probably one of the best places. There was no one answer, you needed hands-on work and you needed someone who could put in the time to do it every day."

It was an interminable wait for Clark. Once he was so discouraged that he told his mother he was going to quit.

"I didn't know what to say," Alma said. "He could barely stand and he couldn't sit in one position for a minute."

"His whole soul, his whole sense of being, relates to playing," Don Meehan said. "To not be able to play, I think, hurt him more than anything. We couldn't get anyone to give us any kind of diagnosis that he needed surgery. It was simply going to be a matter of time."

"That was the year we didn't know if I would play or not," Clark said. "Until we found a guy by the name of Chris Broadhurst, we were spinning our wheels all the time."

Broadhurst, now the Leafs' full-time athletic therapist, had completed a two-year internship in Barrie, Ontario treating chronic back injuries and was now working at the College Park Sports Medicine Centre where he had recently helped Leafs' goalie Ken Wregget rid himself of back problems. When Clark came in for an evaluation in the fall of 1987, Broadhurst began examining his back in earnest. Clark hadn't played since the previous February and if anything his pain was worse.

"It was the whole left side of his body, it was in his arms, his legs, he had trouble taking deep breaths," Broadhurst said. "It always felt like there was a spasm in his back that never went away and it seemed to be getting worse and worse."

Clark wasn't considering whether he could play. By this time, the pain was so severe, his prime concern was living a normal life.

What Broadhurst discovered is that there is nothing structurally wrong with Wendel Clark's back. Clark's high tolerance for pain, ironically, had proven injurious to his health. His back had become the place where old injuries went to fester. Shoulder injuries, brushed aside by Clark in his desire to play, had settled into back problems. His skating stride had been permanently altered by groin injuries that were never given the time to heal.

"When that happened, the body started adapting and changing and Wendel would compensate, the way he shot, the way he skated," Broadhurst said. "Other muscle groups would come in and perform the movements that were to be done. All these compensations started to create compensations through the whole body. Sooner or later, you run out of the adaptive range and he was never able to fight back from the back injury. By that time, the injury compensations were about seven layers deep."

And so Clark and Broadhurst began working on old injuries, separated shoulders, two whiplash injuries, a concussion, a rib injury, a lower back injury suffered in the 1987 Canada Cup as well as some smaller spinal injuries of no fixed time period.

"He had been to some very good people, all the gurus, but the problem was people were looking at the spine as its own entity," Broadhurst said. "It's only when you started working from out to in rather than looking at the spine that you were able to start relieving some of the tensions and pressures."

It was grueling work. The two would meet at the clinic where Broadhurst would often spend three hours a night with Clark on top of his regular practice. Broadhurst used massage and electrical stimulation to kick start the damaged areas. Daily acupuncture minimized the pain of the deep massage that brought blood back into damaged muscles.

"You realize how fun the game is after you've had injuries," Clark said. "There is nothing to the game if you're healthy. You go up to the rink, you practice and you're done. An hour and a half a day. When you're injured, it's not so much the therapy time but the anxiety of, 'What am I going to do now, where am I going to do it and how much time do I have left?' "

Wendel Clark at 22 was a dramatically different person from Wendel Clark at 19. The player who, as a junior, would rather be traded than sit out made himself the player who refused to play until he was able.

"You're 19 years old and you're with the team and you take a lot of pressure in your head," Clark said. "You say, 'I can't let anybody know that I'm hurt or I can't let anybody know I can't play.'

"As you get older, you don't care. 'I'm not going,' that's all you say. 'I'm not practicing today because if you want me to play tomorrow, I'm not practicing today.' You have the experience and you have the respect of people. You make that decision and they're not going to think badly of you."

The residual effects of that period linger with Clark, physically and emotionally. To play, he needs daily therapy that ranges from light stretching to two hours of treatments. He has acupuncture almost every day. He rotates his neck over breakfast and the sound of bones falling back into alignment is jarring. He has permanently poor circulation in his hands, the result of dozens of fights.

"I ache every day, it's a common thing," Clark shrugged. "Every day it's one thing or another."

And so, every day, usually in the warm-up, Clark can tell what he can do that night. Is his shoulder tender? Are his legs heavy? After injuries to both knees, he uses high-tech braces to keep them in alignment. And still he wonders, whenever a new pain appears or an old one returns, how much farther his body will take him.

"You start getting tight, it's, is this going to be the last time you go or not," Clark said. "Every day. It's just something that's part of my game now. That's an ongoing battle."

Clark's list of injuries is a study in anatomy. In 1989, he missed seven games with a bruised muscle above his left knee. He tore ligaments in his right knee in January, 1990, and missed 29 games. A muscle injury in his rib cage cost him

12 more games in February, 1991. In October, 1991, he missed 12 games with partially torn knee ligaments. Two months later, strained knee ligaments forced him out of another 24 games. He missed four games with a groin injury in October, 1992, and 13 games with a strained rib muscle in January, 1993. A bruised foot in December, 1993, meant a 17-game layoff. In September, 1994, Clark was checked by Washington's rookie defenseman Ken Klee and his helmet flew off before his head hit the boards. Clark sat out the rest of the exhibition season but the lockout meant no more lost games. He was ready for the Nordiques' opener.

The Leafs did not win a playoff series from 1988 to 1992 and, even when he managed to play 63 games in 1990–91, Clark scored only 18 goals. In 1987–88, 1988–89 and 1989–90, Clark appeared in only one third of the regular season games. Clark's name, synonymous with punishment, was found more often on the injured lists rather than the scoresheet. When he missed 37 games due to injury in 1991–92, he seemed spent as a player, a victim of injuries.

What no one could see was that, slowly, over the years, Clark was gaining back a measure of the health he had once taken for granted. After nearly two years, his back problems had been corrected. Unlike other high-profile Leafs, his will to play had not been eroded during the Ballard years. The lengthy layoffs and a good relationship with Ballard had spared him.

"Harold and I got along fine," Clark said. "He treated my family very well during the whole time. My parents, my dad and him, probably had more conversations than I did." The Clarks viewed Ballard charitably. Les visited with Ballard just a few days before the Leafs' owner died. Unlike most fans, they had no illusions that the Leafs were a public trust.

"To me, he was a person that did all these things to get the media off what was happening," said Alma. "Sometimes, if the media was on the team, he would do something to get it on him."

Clark thought Ballard owed him nothing more than a pay-cheque. He never criticized the Leafs' Byzantine management style or the sometimes shoddy coaching. When Les told Wendel by phone that he should be fighting less, Wendel asked his father if he signed his paycheque. Les said no. Wendel replied that he would listen only to the people who did.

"The same day Harold made the quote that I was swinging the lead and taking too much time off was the same day he came up to me and said, 'Come back when you're ready to play. I don't really care when you play'," Clark said. "He just said what he did because the media wanted to hear it. That's the way Harold was. He was the best person at getting free advertising. Not all of it was good, but it was his team, he owned it, he could do whatever he wanted."

Ballard died April 9, 1990, and Cliff Fletcher arrived a year later. With their lineup devoid of leadership, the Leafs gam-bled that Clark, despite his injuries, should be the club's four-teenth captain.

Clark said he was honored to be chosen for the C and han-dled himself with characteristic modesty. "I don't think of being a captain as being the captain per se," Clark told the *Toronto Star*. "I have the same sweater, just with a letter on it."

"Wendel didn't say much, but the guy who can lead by example doesn't have to say too much," said Todd Gill, the only current Leaf playing when Clark became captain. "You never got sick of him because he didn't say something just to talk. One of his secrets was if he did say something it needed to be said. He was a very smart individual when it came to things like that."

Clark fit the mold of a Leafs' captain perfectly. While he was soft-spoken, modest and self-effacing in public, Hall of Famer

Red Horner, who retired in 1940, was the last Leafs' captain with as much abrasiveness on the ice. Clark's belligerence was worn down but never erased by the years of injuries and losing. His will to win remained unquestioned.

The captaincy ceremony took place at Maple Leaf Gardens on August 8, 1991, and like Sittler, who presented him with the C, Clark opened his first season as captain with a bang. He scored five goals and added three assists in his first two games. He had at least one point in each of his first eight games but knee injuries robbed Clark of the next 37 games.

On January 2, 1992, Wendel Clark stopped being the best player on the Toronto Maple Leafs. Doug Gilmour had been acquired from the Calgary Flames.

Gilmour scored in the first period of his first game with Toronto and did what Clark by himself could not: he made the Leafs immediately respectable. Although they did not qualify for the post-season, the Leafs went 20–18–2 after Gilmour's arrival.

As Vaive's star had been usurped by Clark, the arrival of Gilmour signaled the end of Clark's tenure as the sole Maple Leafs' hope. But lost in the attention over Gilmour's arrival was the fact that, while both had played about 40 games for the Leafs—Clark played 43 and Gilmour 40—Clark outscored Gilmour 19–15 and didn't miss one of the final 31 games of the regular season.

Still, the Leafs did not make the playoffs for the second season in a row. Since Gilmour's leadership credentials were beyond reproach, the call began for the captain's ouster.

"Like a rusting ICBM in a closed-down Siberian silo, Wendel Clark sits," wrote *Toronto Sun* columnist Jay Greenberg in February, 1993. "His warhead is gone. He doesn't pass the puck, see the ice or pick up his man. His body is too brittle to consistently bump and grind and he cannot be counted on to stay in the lineup. Hanging on for a better deal isn't going to bring more for a player whose value long ago peaked."

Clark was healthy, the 66 games he played in 1992–93 was the most he had played in six seasons, but his lack of defense won him little favor with new coach Pat Burns. From his arrival in 1992, Burns worked to limit people's expectations of Clark.

"Maybe it's unfair to Wendel to expect him to carry such a big load," Burns told the *Toronto Star*. "He's a great team guy and character guy. But maybe right now, he's a role player." Clark spent most of the season on the third line with Peter Zezel and Rob Pearson.

Third-line duty was quite a comedown for the player once considered the franchise savior but if it grated on Clark he never let on.

"Pat is very team-oriented and he's the leader of the pack," Clark said. "He has a great system that wins and keeps his team in the game every night. He's in control and that's the way he runs the team. I was a player, he was the coach, so you do what the coach says."

Clark said Burns had a plan.

"He wanted me to adjust my play, to contain myself. He taught me about playing on good teams, he taught me to play my position better, play more within yourself, try not to do too much and, by doing less, you're doing more."

A rib muscle injury suffered on January 17, 1993, knocked Clark out of the lineup for 13 games, a period in which Gilmour wore the C and scored 22 points. The use of Gilmour as captain during Clark's injury was not lost on observers; the heir apparent had been designated.

In February, 1993, Burns was angered when Clark, still out of the lineup with the rib injury, wasn't ready to play in Tampa Bay after the all-star break. Instead of rehabbing in Toronto,

Clark had spent the break with a group of Leafs holidaying in the Caribbean.

"I'm not mad at Wendel, but I'm upset at the way he handled this," Burns told Toronto newspapers. "It didn't look right. He's the captain of the team and we're fighting for our [play-off] lives."

Clark said he didn't stay for therapy because Broadhurst's advice was rest and light exercise, a regimen he could observe anywhere. The real problem, he said, was that the Lightning beat the Leafs 3–1.

"Basically, we lost and I took the brunt for the loss. But everybody knew I was going south for the all-star break. There was nothing I could do for my injury at home, just rest, so whether I rested at home or in the Caribbean, it didn't matter.

"But in a way, that's the way Pat Burns coached, that's his way of getting the team going. He cuts me down, the whole team sees it and goes, 'Oh, he's mad.' I may feel the brunt of it but the whole team feels it and in the long run, it might help the team win."

Clark was by then the subject of almost daily trade rumors. In 1990, he was said to be heading to Montreal for Shayne Corson and Claude Lemieux. Then Clark, along with Rob Pearson, was purported to be on his way to Edmonton for Esa Tikkanen and Joe Murphy. "All Glen [Sather] had to do was say yes," an Oilers' source said, "but we were scared of his back problems."

But Fletcher said trade talks never went past preliminary discussions. "We were never at the stage [with the Oilers] where anything was going to be done," Fletcher told the media. "Wendel Clark can still be an important player for us."

In 1992–93, because of Fletcher's judicious trades, Burns had a much better team than his predecessors to work with. The acquisition of Gilmour as well as Dave Andreychuk from Buffalo were key but so too were quieter transactions such as landing Bill Berg from the New York Islanders and Sylvain Lefebvre from Montreal. Felix Potvin graduated from the minors to become the starting goaltender and Burns drove the Leafs to a 44-win, 99-point season and a first-round showdown with the powerhouse Detroit Red Wings.

The first two games of the series with the Red Wings are close to the lowest points of Clark's career. He hadn't scored in his final ten regular season games and the Leafs, who had built up fan expectations with their record points total, were run over in Detroit, 6–3 and 6–2. Clark's impact, along with several other Leafs', was minimal. Burns barely used Clark in the third period of the second game and the Red Wings physically overpowered the Leafs. Bob Probert had accused Clark of being unwilling to fight on the road, prompting a Detroit writer to paraphrase Probert and say Clark was Wendel at home but "Wendy" on the road.

Probert's remarks fed into the long-held rumor that Clark, a bachelor, is gay. Clark, his agents, his parents and his teammates say he is not. (He would announce his engagement to a Toronto woman in June of 1995.)

But these rumors would provide the unspoken backdrop when the *Toronto Star*'s Rosie DiManno and the *Toronto Sun*'s Christie Blatchford laid the blame for the Leafs' dreadful showing in Detroit on Clark.

On the surface, the criticisms were standard. Clark was the captain and he had played poorly. That Burns had ordered Clark not to fight because he needed his scoring ability to combat far superior Detroit firepower was something neither columnist had any way of knowing.

But it was the viciousness of the criticism, the linking of Clark's performance with his sexuality, the use, intentional or otherwise, of Probert's "Wendy" remark as a code for gay, that stunned even media onlookers.

"On what was a viciously ugly night at the Joe Louis Arena, Wendel Clark had been the prettiest boy on the ice," wrote DiManno.

Blatchford was more to the point.

"There are different definitions of manhood, and of courage, and by one set of standards—the harsh machismo that is the currency of hockey—Wendel Clark was emasculated last night," she wrote.

Clark, recalling the incident over breakfast, just shrugged. "We lost, I had been there the longest and I was the captain of the team. In a way, you may be blaming one player for the whole team playing bad but that's part of being the captain. You're going to take heat. It always gets personal in the media. There's so many writers and so many TV cameras, there's only so many things to cover. They run out of stories and they have to cover something so they get personal."

Clark said he had no quarrel with Probert or the reporters. "Players were making quotes in papers. You're in the middle of a heated battle in the series; players are going to do anything to get an edge. That's what hockey is all about, or sports. If you can throw a player off his game you're going to win."

Many other Leafs weren't so forgiving. "Personally, I think it was a gutless move on the media's part," said defenseman Todd Gill. "It was gutless to chastise him, yet he came back and won that series for us and the series after that. Then he almost single-handedly won game six for us in L.A."

The Leafs won the next two games at home with Clark the first star in game three with a goal and an assist. In game four, Clark scored twice in a 3–2 overtime win.

Suddenly, after almost two decades of uninterrupted despair, the Toronto Maple Leafs were Stanley Cup contenders and Clark was again their leader.

The Leafs defeated both the Red Wings and the Blues in

seven games before they fell to Los Angeles in another seven-game series. Clark played magnificently. He had ten goals and 20 points in the 21 games, including five in the final three games against Los Angeles. When Gilmour was elbowed by Marty McSorley late in the Los Angeles series, it was Clark who instantly fought the towering King to re-establish Gilmour's untouchability.

Clark said the criticism had no impact on his performance in the Detroit series despite his sudden rise to hero status after the Wendy fiasco.

"I don't think I played any different the first two than I did the last five. I think, as a team, we played better. Just like I don't think anyone worked less hard in the first two games than in the last five but we played smarter as a team in the last five."

Others felt the criticism was wounding. "He knew that he was doing the best he could and that certain things that were expected of him may have been unreasonable," Don Meehan said. "I know personally that he was terribly hurt but he would never convey that publicly."

Burns conceded that Clark got better as the series evolved. But he too thought linking Clark's on-ice performance with his personal life was ridiculous.

"You can question Wendel's ability to score, you can question his ability to shoot. But nobody will ever question Wendel's toughness, will question Wendel's heart or will question whether he wants to play the game or not. That's bull."

"He played like a man possessed," said Leafs' general manager Cliff Fletcher. "Wendel's the captain of the Toronto Maple Leafs."

The 1993–94 season, his final year as the Leafs' captain, was Clark's finest professional campaign. He scored 46 goals in 64 games, eight of them game-winners. The game he had been piecing together for years finally took shape, his reputation was so solid he was rarely bothered and the extra space he enjoyed on the ice was rarely challenged. Clark accrued only 115 penalty minutes.

"When you're younger, you're invincible. I still think the same way as when I was younger but now I pick my spots better. When you were 18 it didn't matter how big the guy was."

Clark even began to show creativity on the attack. No longer were his shot and a drive to the net the only weapons in his arsenal. Restored to good health, Clark averaged 0.72 goals per game. Only Pavel Bure and Cam Neely did better. The trade rumors were forgotten and Toronto fans vigorously cheered their captain.

The Leafs again advanced to the semi-finals and Clark was the club's leading goal scorer with nine goals. Seven of them, including a game winner, came in a narrow seven-game victory over San Jose but Clark could manage only one goal in the five-game conference final loss to Vancouver.

Then came draft day, June 28, and the deal; Clark, Lefebvre, premier prospect Landon Wilson and a draft choice for Sundin, Garth Butcher, Todd Warriner and a draft choice. Discussions were initiated a month before, on the day Pierre Lacroix became the general manager of the Québec Nordiques. The Nordiques' initial and most pressing need was defense. They wanted Lefebvre and they were able to offer Sundin as a lure. Québec, with the imminent arrival of Swedish star Peter Forsberg, were overendowed with centers. Sundin was exceptionally talented but he had pouted and played ineffectively the season before when the Nordiques had refused to renegotiate his contract.

Clark's was the next name to surface since, aside from defense, the Nordiques' greatest need was for an established character player. Clark's credentials were impeccable. The rest of the deal fell into place over the next few weeks.

Fletcher notified Clark by phone.

"You knew something was going to happen but I didn't know who, what or when," Clark recalled. "It could be me, it could be anybody. There were no rumors that I heard. Before that, every summer there were rumors."

Clark managed his departure from Toronto as decently as he had his entrance. When Don Meehan suggested renegotiating his contract with the Nordiques, Clark vetoed the idea.

To Clark, the issue was simple. He had signed a contract. No one had taken his money back when he was injured, and he would not ask for more now that he was not.

"I had no reason to renegotiate. Coming here this year, if the team does well, you can always remind the team of what happened. 'I never rocked the boat. I did everything you asked me to do. I was positive.'

"Down the road, you can collect on that, maybe. You do it up front, the owners have resentment toward you because you rocked the boat early, you scared them. Make them feel comfortable early. If they're good people, they'll reward you later."

"I think he impressed a lot of people when he got traded," said Lefebvre. "He didn't complain. He just showed up and said I'm going to be part of the Nordiques now. The only thing he wanted was to play hockey."

"Finally," wrote a signmaker in Clark's first game at the Colisée. "We have a soul."

Clark immediately became an assistant captain of the Nordiques and the Toronto media speculated that he would succeed Joe Sakic as captain. Clark said the rumor was just that.

"It's Joe's team," Clark said simply. "That other stuff was just media stuff."

Clark's impact was felt almost immediately. The Nordiques roared out of the gate and Clark's linemate, Sakic, enjoyed a remarkable start. Sakic, a prodigiously talented player, played the best hockey of his career with Clark on his left and the Nordiques finished first overall.

"Basically, people are scared of him," said Sakic. "He's got that reputation and he makes a lot of room for himself."

The kind of leadership Wendel Clark provides is difficult to quantify. It's not just scoring big goals and it can't be manufactured. It's being genuine and it's being smart and it's being yourself, not just on the ice but on the bus, in the trainer's room and in a restaurant. For Wendel Clark, it's being Wendel Clark, the genuine article.

"I don't try to lead," said Clark. "I just try to go out and deal with situations the best way I know how."

A decade after arriving in Toronto, Wendel Clark still wears the belt buckle, the one that says "Just a Farmer."

At the press conference on Canada Day, a reporter asked Clark if his habit of answering long-winded questions with a few words would ever die, if the kid from Kelvington would ever change.

Clark looked the questioner squarely in the eye.

"No," was all he said.

POSTSCRIPT

Friday, May 19, 1995

Doug Gilmour sat at his stall, completely dressed save for his battered feet which he propped on a stool.

The room was quiet in the wake of the Leafs' 5–2 loss in game seven of their first-round series. There seemed no urgency to finish anything.

So much had changed in a year. Chicago Stadium, the site of the Leafs' series-clinching victory a year earlier, was a heap of rubble only yards away. The Hawks' home was now the sparkling new United Center, a plush building that possessed many more amenities but had nowhere near the atmosphere of the club's former arena.

In ruins too was the Leafs' dream of a third consecutive trip to the Stanley Cup final four and the untarnished glow Gilmour had enjoyed as the team's best player.

"This is a season," Gilmour said, "I just want to forget."

We are never as human as when we fail, and the cloak of invincibility that protected Doug Gilmour in his first two seasons with the Maple Leafs evaporated in 1994–95. The heartbreak of the 1994 playoffs blended into disappointment in the autumn as the owners' lockout shelved the season for over 100 days. His trip to Switzerland had been a failure; Gilmour improved neither his conditioning nor his game overseas.

Injuries hounded him all season. His feet often went numb and he played with a sore back for the final month of the regular season and the playoffs. Along the way his nose was hit by a shot and broken and he injured his neck.

The emergence of Mats Sundin as a Leafs' star affected Gilmour's ice time. He spent the latter stages of the season and some of the playoffs playing on a line with tough guy Tie Domi. The decision by Leafs' coach Pat Burns to remove Gilmour from the penalty killing unit was designed to spare him wear and tear but the ultimate result was to deprive him of five or six minutes of extra ice time a night, ice time Gilmour felt he needed to remain sharp.

During the playoffs, the calls for improved play reached a crescendo. "Will the Real Doug Gilmour Please Stand Up," blared a headline in the *Toronto Sun*.

The criticism stung. "I was disappointed," Gilmour said later, "but I've been criticized in other cities too."

The game that Gilmour had struggled so hard to assemble finally seemed to be coming together in the later games of the Chicago series. Gilmour finished the playoffs second on the team with six points, all assists. In the final three games, he delivered more consistent flashes of the Gilmour of old than he had all season, but it was too late. The Leafs, undermined by a drastically weakened defense with the departures of Sylvain Lefebvre and Bob Rouse, were never more than a shadow of their previous selves. Even if Gilmour could have rekindled the fire of the past, it would not have been enough.

But the question lingered through the summer: Had Doug Gilmour been playing too hard for too many years?

Gilmour said he wasn't slipping. "I think I'll retire before I slip. If I get the opportunity to play the way I want to, I'll be OK."

Gilmour said he remained a conscientious player defensively, even if his offense was on sabbatical. "A lot of times if you want to evaluate a team, you do it by looking at the numbers. I guess if you only go by that, I didn't play that well."

Doug Gilmour's career is far from over. At 32, he has productive years ahead of him and, if his tenure as a 100-point man is past, his stint as a premier two-way player is not. Players frequently suffer off-years in their early thirties, and then redefine their role in the game and prosper for several more seasons.

If the latter stages of the Chicago series proved anything, it was that the game seems ready to return to Gilmour. He began making the right play more automatically. After all, his career was built on fiercely attacking any challenge put in his way.

The fate of the team he will captain seems the more important issue. Rumors began swirling in the playoffs that coach Pat Burns would leave the club to coach the Los Angeles Kings, and the club's age is a pressing concern. The Maple Leafs lost their best prospect, Landon Wilson, in the Wendel Clark deal and 13 players will be 30 or over in the 1995–96 season. Veteran rearguards Jamie Macoun (34) and Garth Butcher (33) and 35-year-old right-winger Mike Gartner seem near the end of their careers. The Leafs do have three exceptional young players they can build on: Sundin, Felix Potvin and defenseman Kenny Johnson.

Any dramatic infusion of talent is probably going to come via trades. There was talk of signing a big-name free agent such as New Jersey defenseman Scott Stevens.

But all these were questions for another day. Right now, defeat was too recent. Doug Gilmour got up and put on his shoes. It was time to move on.

WHERE ARE THEY NOW?

Hap Day (1927–37): The most successful coach in Maple Leafs' history was also one of their best captains. Day died in his sleep in 1990.

Charlie Conacher (1937–38): In 1941 Conacher retired to the oil business after playing out the string with Detroit and the New York Americans. He died in 1967.

Red Horner (1938–40): The toughest defenseman in team history, Red Horner remains an impossible man to keep down. He spent the past winter recovering from surgery that gave him an artificial knee. At 86, he is in excellent health and lives in Toronto.

Syl Apps (1940–43, 1945–48): Apps remains outside the public eye in his Kingston condominium. In January 1995, family and friends feted him with an eightieth birthday party.

Bob Davidson (1943–45): Davidson retired from hockey in the late 1980s. One of the greatest judges of talent anywhere, the 82-year-old former Leafs' head scout lives in Leaside in Toronto.

Ted Kennedy (1948–55, 1956–57): Kennedy, perhaps the most inspirational captain, lives in Niagara-on-the-Lake, Ontario, and continues to work as the director of security at the Fort Erie Race Track. At 69, he is very active in the club's alumni functions.

Sid Smith (1955–56): Smith played a dozen years for the Leafs but left the club in 1958. He was the player-coach of the world champion Whitby Dunlops and retired to private business in the early 1960s. Now 70, Smith is semi-retired and lives in Newmarket, Ontario, where he works part-time at the city's courthouse.

Jim Thomson (1956–57): Thomson, one of the finest defensive defenseman ever, was traded to the Chicago Blackhawks in 1957, largely because of his involvement with the players' union. He died in May, 1992 at the age of 68.

George Armstrong (1957–69): Armstrong captained the Maple Leafs for 12 seasons, a league record, and remains with the club as a scout. He turned 65 on July 6, 1995.

Dave Keon (1969–75): The last member of the Leafs' 1967 championship team to play in the NHL, Keon has been retired for 13 years but remains extremely popular with Leafs' fans. At 55, he is semi-retired and lives in Palm Beach Gardens, Florida.

Darryl Sittler (1975–81): Sittler, 45, works as an assistant to Leafs' general manager Cliff Fletcher but his position is basically public relations. His son Ryan is a prospect in the Philadelphia Flyers' organization. Sittler lives in Amherst, New York.

Rick Vaive (1981–86): The 1995 post-season was not kind to Maple Leaf captains past and present. Vaive's South Carolina

Stingrays were swept 3–0 in the first round of the East Coast Hockey League playoffs. He is 36.

Rob Ramage (1989–91): Ramage, who had played with Colorado, St. Louis and Calgary before arriving in Toronto in 1989, continued his tour of the hockey universe after being released by the Leafs in the expansion draft in June, 1992. He played in Minnesota and Tampa Bay, won a Stanley Cup in 1993 as a member of the Montreal Canadiens and finished his career in Philadelphia in 1994. Now 36, he works as a stockbroker in St. Louis.

Wendel Clark (1991–94): In 1994–95, the 29-year-old Clark scored 12 goals in 37 regular season games and was criticized when his Quebec Nordiques fell in six games to the New York Rangers. The club bolted Quebec City for Denver on May 25, 1995.

Doug Gilmour (1994–present): Gilmour, 32, finished the regular season with 10 goals and recorded 33 points in 44 games. He was held goal-less in the post-season for the first time in his 12-year career.

INDEX